CANADIAN
SOCIAL STUDIES
HOMEWORK

EVERYTHING YOU NEED TO KNOW ABOUT

CANADIAN
SOCIAL STUDIES
HOMEWORK

ANNE ZEMAN

KATE KELLY

Scholastic Canada Ltd.
Toronto New York London Auckland Sydney
Mexico City New Delhi Hong Kong Buenos Aires

Scholastic Canada Ltd.
604 King Street West, Toronto, Ontario M5V 1E1, Canada

Scholastic Inc.
557 Broadway, New York, NY 10012, USA

Scholastic Australia Pty Limited
PO Box 579, Gosford, NSW 2250, Australia

Scholastic New Zealand Limited
Private Bag 94407, Greenmount, Auckland, New Zealand

Scholastic Ltd.
Villiers House, Clarendon Avenue, Leamington Spa,
Warwickshire CV32 5PR, UK

Interior design, Bennett Gewirtz, Gewirtz Graphics, Inc. Interior illustration, Greg Paprocki.
Photographs courtesy of the Canadian Heritage Gallery and the National Archives of Canada:
Page 6, CHG #10034/NAC #C-13470; page 13, CHG #10046/NAC #PA-29120; page 23,
CHG #20049, NAC #C-103059; page 30, CHG #10162/NAC #C-11250; page 33,
CHG #10210, NAC #C-137346; page 89, CHG #10095, NAC #C-37125; page 91,
CHG #10095/NAC #C-37125
Photographs courtesy of the Canadian Heritage Gallery:
Page 37, CHG #20697; page 42, CHG #219143
Photographs courtesy of iStockphoto:
Page 72, Natalia Bratslavsky; page 74, Hubert White; page 46, Pierrette Guertin;
page 78, Melissa King; page 80; page 82, Sang Nguyen; page 84, Edzard de Ranitz;
page 86, Cezar Serbanescu; page 88, Lauri Wiberg
Photo page 50 courtesy of the Library of Congress
Photo page 58 courtesy of the Scholastic Picture Research Department

Library and Archives Canada Cataloguing in Publication
Zeman, Anne, 1952-

Everything you need to know about Canadian social studies homework
/Anne Zeman, Kate Kelly.

Co-published by Irving Place Press.
Fourth to sixth grades.

ISBN 0-439-95233-6

1. Social sciences—Canada—Study and teaching—Handbooks, manuals, etc.—Juvenile literature.
2. Homework—Handbooks, manuals, etc.—Juvenile literature. I. Kelly, Kate II. Title.

LB1584.5.C3Z44 2005   j300'.971   C2005-900600-5

6 5 4 3 2 1   Printed in Canada   06 07 08 09 10

Contents

Introduction

It's time to do your homework—but you have questions. You need some help, but no adults are around, and you can't reach your classmates on the phone. Where can you go for help?

What Questions Does This Book Answer?

In *Everything You Need to Know About Canadian Social Studies Homework*, you will find a wealth of information, including answers to some of the most commonly asked Canadian Social Studies homework questions, such as:

- What was Pangaea, and what do it and continental drift have to do with Earth's continents? Find out on page 2.

- What was the League of Five Nations? To learn more about the League and its Iroquoian members, see page 8.

- What new land did John Cabot find? You can read more about Cabot and other European explorers on pages 15–20.

- Who fought in the Rebellions of 1837? What were the rebels' motives and what did they hope to gain? The answers can be found on pages 37–40.

- What were the Charlottetown and Quebec Conferences? Learn how important they were to Canadian Confederation on page 43.

- Why did World War I start, and how did Canada distinguish itself? The answers are on pages 49–53.

- What caused the Great Depression, and how did it end? The Great Depression is the topic of page 56.

- Where can you find the highest point in Canada? What's Canada's newest territory? Take a tour of Canada's provinces on pages 66–93 and find out.

- Who is Canada's Head of State? Turn to page 94 — the answer might surprise you.

- Who chooses the members of the Supreme Court? You can find more information on Canada's judicial system on pages 101–102.

What Is the *Everything You Need to Know About...Homework* series?

The *Everything You Need to Know About...Homework* series is a set of unique reference resources written especially to answer the homework questions of fourth, fifth, and sixth graders. The series provides information to answer commonly asked homework questions in a variety of subjects. Here you'll find facts, charts, definitions, and explanations, complete with examples and illustrations that will supplement schoolwork colourfully, clearly, and comprehensively.

A Note to Parents

It's important to support your children's efforts to do homework. Welcome their questions, and see that they have access to a well-lighted desk or table, pencils, paper, and any other books or equipment that they need—such as rulers, calculators, reference books or textbooks, and so on. You might also set aside a special time each day for doing homework, a time when you're available to answer questions that may arise. But don't do your children's homework for them. Remember, homework should create a bond between school and home. It is meant to enhance the lessons taught at school on a daily basis, and to promote good work and study habits. Although it is gratifying to have your children present flawless homework papers, the flawlessness should be a result of your children's explorations and efforts—not your own.

The Scholastic Homework Reference series is designed to help your children complete their homework on their own to the best of their abilities. If they're stuck, you can use these books with them to help find answers to troubling homework problems. And remember, when the work is done, praise your children for a job well done.

Canada

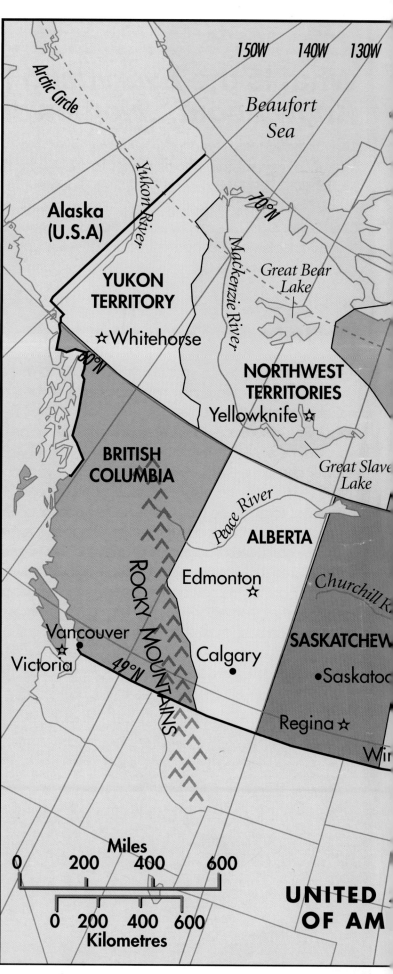

150W   140W   130W

Arctic Circle

Beaufort
Sea

Alaska
(U.S.A)

70°N

Yukon River

YUKON
TERRITORY

Mackenzie River

Great Bear
Lake

☆Whitehorse

60°N

NORTHWEST
TERRITORIES

Yellowknife ☆

BRITISH
COLUMBIA

Great Slave
Lake

Peace River

ALBERTA

Churchill R.

ROCKY MOUNTAINS

Edmonton
☆

Vancouver
Victoria ☆

Calgary
●

SASKATCHEW

●Saskatoo

49°N

Regina ☆

Win

Miles
0   200   400   600

0   200   400   600
Kilometres

UNITED
OF AM

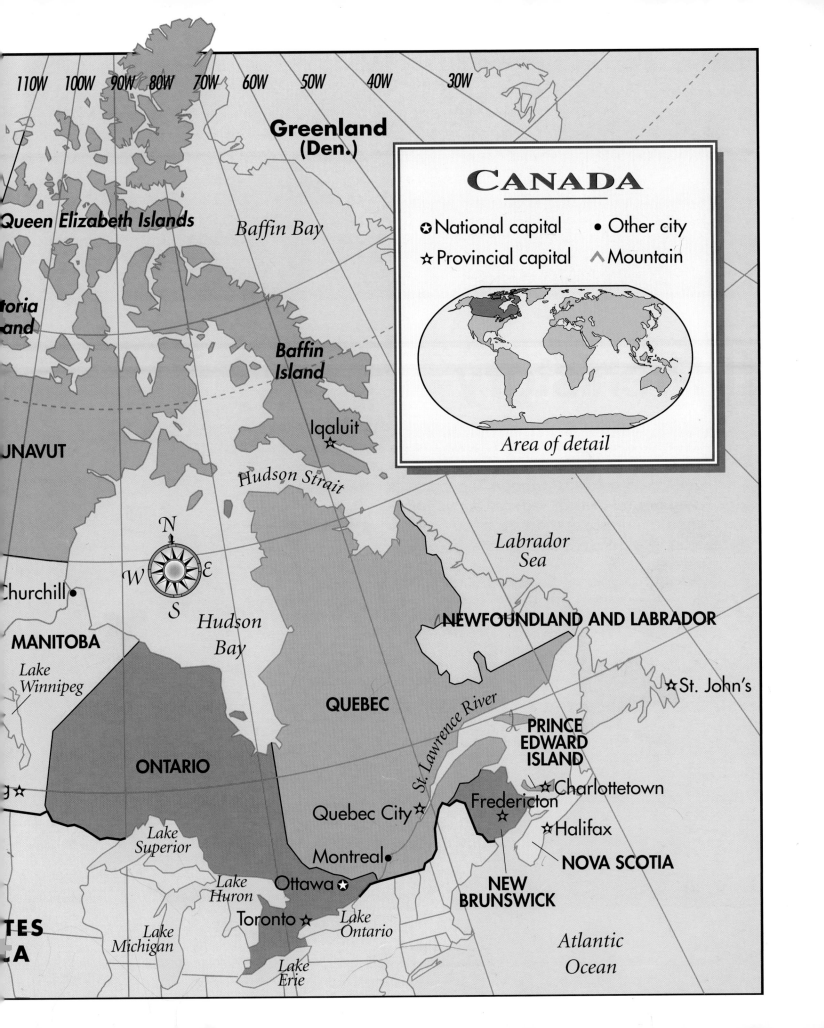

110W 100W 90W 80W 70W 60W 50W 40W 30W

**Greenland
(Den.)**

Queen Elizabeth Islands

Baffin Bay

*toria
and*

*Baffin
Island*

NUNAVUT

Iqaluit
☆

Hudson Strait

N
W ● E
S

*Hudson
Bay*

*Labrador
Sea*

NEWFOUNDLAND AND LABRADOR

Churchill ●

MANITOBA

*Lake
Winnipeg*

QUEBEC

☆ St. John's

**PRINCE
EDWARD
ISLAND**

ONTARIO

St. Lawrence River

☆ Charlottetown

Fredericton
☆

g ☆

*Lake
Superior*

Quebec City ☆

☆ Halifax

NOVA SCOTIA

Montreal ●

**NEW
BRUNSWICK**

TES

LA

*Lake
Huron*

Ottawa ✪

*Lake
Michigan*

Toronto ☆

*Lake
Ontario*

*Atlantic
Ocean*

*Lake
Erie*

CANADA

✪ National capital   ● Other city

☆ Provincial capital   ⌃ Mountain

Area of detail

Chapter **1**

Prehistory

Canada occupies more than 9.9 million square kilometres of the North American continent. Scientists believe this large land mass came into being more than 200 million years ago, when all the continents of the world were connected in a supercontinent called **Pangaea**. The continents, in a movement called **continental drift**, moved apart along **fault lines** in the Pangaea land mass, creating the layout of land and oceans that make up the earth today.

Europe Asia

North
America

PANGAEA

Africa

India

South America

Australia

Antarctica

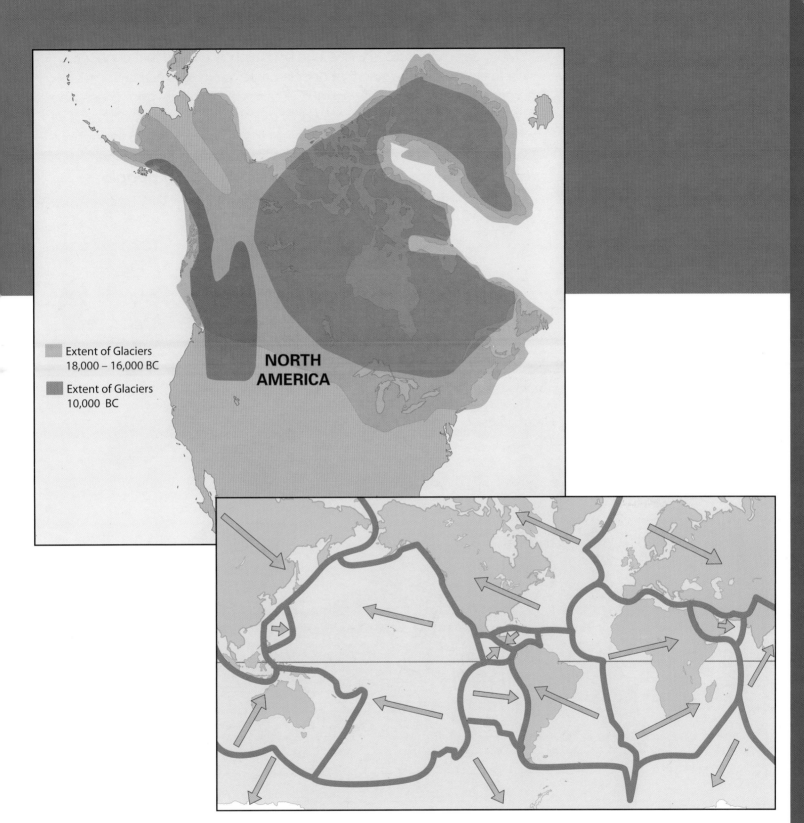

Extent of Glaciers
18,000 – 16,000 BC

Extent of Glaciers
10,000 BC

NORTH
AMERICA

The shape of the North American land mass is due in large part to fault lines in the earth's **tectonic plates**. The **topography**, or the physical features on the land—mountains, valleys, plateaus, plains, rivers, lakes, and so on—is a result of tectonics and **glaciation**, which is the movement of huge, slow-moving sheets of ice that scientists believe covered the continent approximately 20,000 and 12,000 years ago.

3

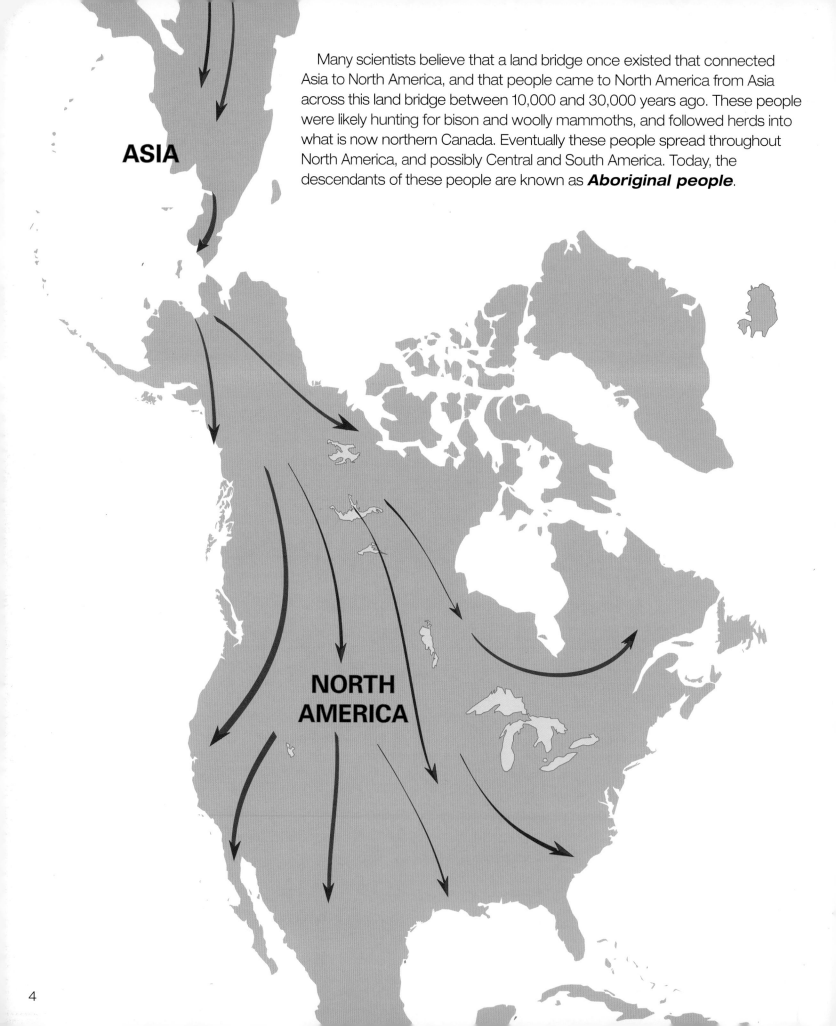

Many scientists believe that a land bridge once existed that connected Asia to North America, and that people came to North America from Asia across this land bridge between 10,000 and 30,000 years ago. These people were likely hunting for bison and woolly mammoths, and followed herds into what is now northern Canada. Eventually these people spread throughout North America, and possibly Central and South America. Today, the descendants of these people are known as **Aboriginal people**.

ASIA

NORTH AMERICA

Aboriginal Peoples

Archaeological findings suggest that Asian hunters inhabited North America more than 10,000 years ago. These early peoples spread out and established themselves across the continent long before the arrival of the Europeans. By the time of European contact (see p. 6), Aboriginal peoples had developed more than 50 distinct languages and a variety of separate cultures.

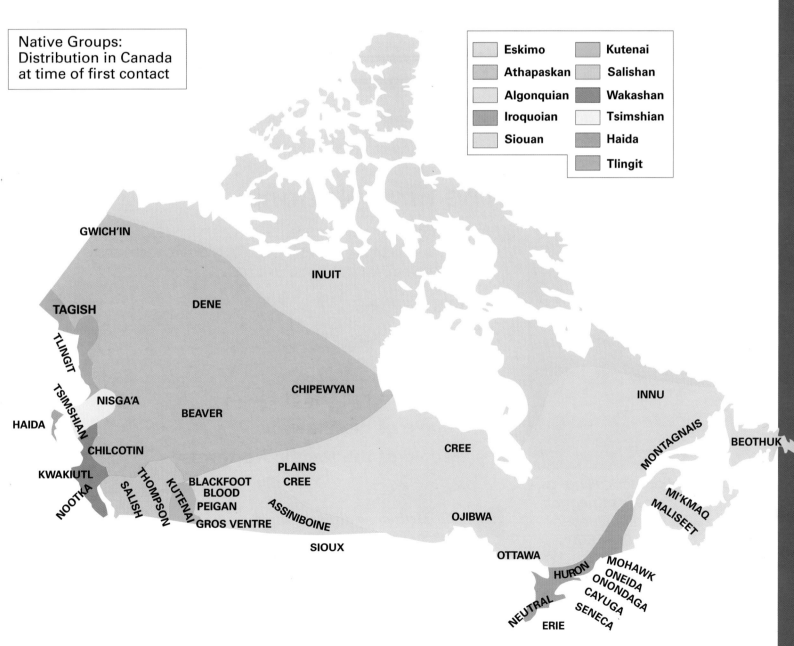

Native Groups: Distribution in Canada at time of first contact

Eskimo	Kutenai
Athapaskan	Salishan
Algonquian	Wakashan
Iroquoian	Tsimshian
Siouan	Haida
	Tlingit

Most scholars agree that at the time of first contact approximately 500,000 Aboriginal people lived in the lands that make up present-day Canada.

Defining First Contact

The contact between Aboriginal peoples and Europeans did not happen all in one place or all at one time. For example, contact between Europeans and Inuit people in the Arctic region can be traced back more than 1,000 years, but contact with other Aboriginal groups for only 400–500 years. At first, contact was made mainly for trade, but it had a greater impact than a simple swap of food and other goods.

THE PRODUCTS OF CONTACT

1 New, foreign items are traded within long-established Aboriginal trading networks.

2 New diseases are spread among Aboriginal people.

3 European cast-offs and artifacts are left by European explorers and adapted by Aboriginal peoples for use as tools, clothing, or weapons.

An Aboriginal hunter calling, as depicted by Cornelius Krieghoff, an artist who lived in Quebec from the 1840s to the 1860s.

The First Nations

First Nations is a term that came into use in the 1970s to describe some of the Aboriginal peoples in Canada. The term varies and is often used to describe the following distinct cultural groups.

1 Algonquians

2 Athapaskans

3 Iroquois

4 People of the Great Plains

5 People of the Plateau

6 People of the Pacific Northwest

The Métis are a distinct cultural group that emerged in what is now central Canada. The Métis are people descended from mixed European (mostly French Canadian) and Aboriginal ancestry. The Inuit are also distinct from First Nations peoples. The term Aboriginal peoples includes all three groups.

An eastern Algonquian family of the 1860s, travelling in the Quebec winter by toboggan and snowshoes.

The Algonquians

At the time of first contact, the Algonquians—including the Cree, Ojibwa, and Ottawa (woodlands), and the Maliseet and Mi'kmaq (coast)—lived mainly in the forests of the Canadian Shield. Called the "People of the North Woods," the Algonquians moved around in kinship bands and lived in wigwams made of bent wooden poles and bark or skins. A wigwam held one or two families and could be built very quickly with materials readily available on the forest floor.

The Athapaskans

The Athapaskans—including the Kutchin, Dogrib, Beaver, Slavey, and Chipewyan—are also called the Dene. Like the Algonquians, Athapaskan people were semi-nomadic hunters and fishers whose main food sources were the large and small game animals of the boreal forests of the subarctic northwest. Also like the Algonquians, the Athapaskans participated in inland fur trading, as well as in coastal fishing.

The Athapaskan language group is distinct from Algonquian, however, and their homeland far distant. Unlike the Algonquians, the Athapaskans appear to have been among the last Aboriginal groups to deal directly with Europeans. This is in part because of the structure of Aboriginal trading alliances, and in part because Europeans did not come into regular, direct contact with the Athapaskans until the expansion of the Hudson's Bay Company and its rival, the North West Company, in the late 1700s. By 1790, the Chipewyans began to trade directly with Europeans, often bartering for higher prices between the two rival firms.

From 1821 to 1858, the Hudson's Bay Company controlled all trade in the subarctic region. During this period, as their land became over-hunted, the Athapaskans came to depend more and more on the Europeans for food and goods.

The Mi'kmaq of the Maritimes

Speakers of Algonquian languages also lived far from the woodlands, as far east, in fact, as the Atlantic provinces. Among the eastern Algonquian speakers were the Mi'kmaq, who lived in semi-nomadic communities ranging from the Gaspé Peninsula to Nova Scotia to Newfoundland. Traders and middlemen, the Mi'kmaq were among the first tribes to trade with the French, with whom they remained staunch allies against the British. A bounty dated from 1756 offers 25 pounds from "His Majesty's Government" in exchange for a Mi'kmaq scalp.

Today the Iroquois call themselves the Haudenausanee, "people of the longhouse."

The Iroquois

The Iroquois lived in the St. Lawrence-Great Lakes region. They were farmers who grew, among other foods, corn, beans, and squash. The Iroquoians lived in longhouses, some more than 100 metres in length, that would be home to as many as 50 people. Longhouses were built within fortified towns. Outside the towns were large community fields. Among the Iroquoians are the Huron, Neutrals, Erie, Mohawk, Oneida, Onondaga, Cayuga, Seneca, and Tuscarora peoples.

The Oldest Democracy in North America

Five Iroquois nations—the Mohawk, Oneida, Onondaga, Cayuga, and Seneca—formed a confederacy called the League of Five Nations around 1451. This confederacy has been called the oldest democracy in North America. A sixth nation, the Tuscarora, joined the confederacy in 1722. Also known as The Great Law of Peace, the Iroquois Confederacy was, according to legend, inspired by two elders—Dekanahwideh and Hiawatha—who called upon the warring Iroquois to make peace and enter into a union like the families in the longhouse. As a symbol of the confederacy, a great white pine tree with its roots and canopy spreading out in peace in all directions was planted. Some legends say it was planted on top of a war club. Sometimes called "the Romans of the New World," the five nations of the Iroquois Confederacy ultimately overran their neighbours—including the Huron, Neutral, and Erie—and slowed the spread of French influence and settlement along the St. Lawrence. The Confederacy was ultimately torn apart by the American Revolution, when:

1. The Mohawk and most of the Seneca sided with the British.

2. Some of the Tuscarora and the Oneida sided with the Americans.

3. The Onondaga and Cayuga, at first neutral, later joined the Mohawk and Seneca on the British side (see p. 27).

False Faces

False faces—Iroquoian masks carved directly into tree trunks and then removed from the living wood—are significant items in healing rituals. These masks represent good spirits with the ability to cure a variety of ailments. Despite this serious purpose, the masks themselves often appear comical, with crooked noses and bulging lips. False faces have religious significance among Iroquois to this day and are still used in traditional ceremonies.

Longhouse Living

The Iroquois lived in longhouses that had an opening at one end and a central passageway. Multiple families lived in the same dwelling.

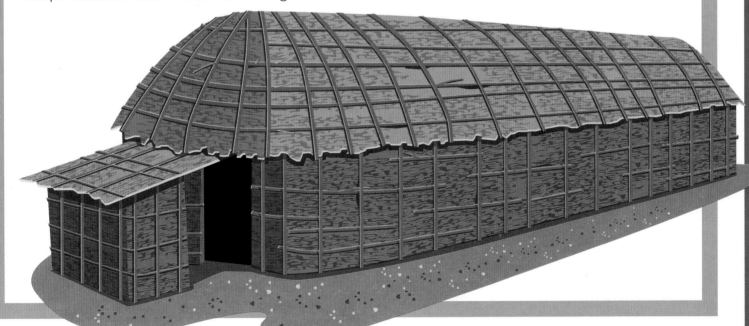

People of the Great Plains

The People of the Great Plains were widely known as great horsemen and warriors. Although horses existed in prehistoric North America, they are thought to have been hunted into extinction. Later, Spanish explorers traded horses to southern Aboriginal groups who, by the mid-1700s, traded them to northern groups, including the Sioux (Dakota/Lakota), Crow, Cree, Assiniboine, and Blackfoot. For more than a century, the People of the Plains, with their "horse-powered" mobility and speed, became a powerful presence in the western grasslands.

The Plains people were primarily nomadic hunters. They lived in teepees, portable tents made of buffalo hides draped across raised poles. Teepees could be put up and taken down very quickly. For the most part, these hunters followed the buffalo (more correctly, the North American bison), which provided not only food, but also clothing, blankets, housing, and tools.

The Plains people were ingenious in their hunting methods. Not only did they take buffalo by riding beside them and shooting them with bows and arrows, but also by corralling the animals into gradually narrowing fenced areas. Buffalo were also driven off cliffs. At a cliff site in southwestern Alberta, called Head-Smashed-In Buffalo Jump, is a boneyard dating back more than 5,000 years. Buffalo bones up to 10 metres deep still lie there.

Buffalo: Everything But the Bellow

The People of the Plains wasted none of the buffalo. You could say that they used everything but the bison's bellow.

Hide: Tanned for use as clothing, moccasins, and shelter

Shoulder Bones: Used as shovels

Rib Bones: Handles for knives and other tools

Bladder: Water container

Stomach: Containers

Leg Bones: Used as tools for tanning skins

Hoof: Decoration or jewellery

Teeth: Decoration or jewellery

Toe Bones: Games for children, and used in games of chance

Hair: Ropes, fly swatters; tail used for small whips

Medicine Wheels

The Great Plains are dotted with thousands of stone markers that the Europeans called "medicine wheels." These circular patterns of stone in the grass appear to have been used for a variety of purposes, such as marking battlefields or ceremonial grounds. Many date back thousands of years. As many as 150 medicine wheels have been located in North America, and 125 have been found in southern Saskatchewan and Alberta.

A handmade medicine wheel.

People of the Plateau

Before European contact, two very different nations called the high plateau of British Columbia home: the Interior Salish, who may have been pushed there from the west coast, and the Kutenai, who may have originally lived on the Great Plains.

The Interior Salish travelled with the season, spending much of late summer and early autumn fishing for the salmon that played an important role in their economy. Along with hunting and plant gathering, fishing helped feed the people through the winter.

During the summer the Interior Salish lived in simple dwellings made of bark over poles, but in the winter they lived in earthen houses dug into the ground, with entrances at the top or sides.

The language of the Kutenai is entirely different from that of their neighbours—or, for that matter, from any known Aboriginal nation. The upper Kutenai hunted big game, like deer and elk, and crossed the mountains every few months to hunt bison. The lower Kutenai, who lived down river, hunted smaller game, including ducks and fish.

Ogopogo

The Interior Salish tell the tale of N'ha-A-Itk, a monster who dwells in the depths of Okanagan Lake and pulls fishermen to their death in the icy waters. N'ha-A-Itk is better known today as Ogopogo. Legend says that this monster was so feared and revered by Aboriginal people that sacrifices of small animals were made to the creature to distract it from Salish fishermen.

Totem Poles

Totem poles tell the history of clans. They can serve as a coat-of-arms, as well as a symbol of wealth. The greater the number and size of poles, the greater a clan's wealth.

Totem poles may have originated with the Tsimshian and were later refined by the Kwakiutl. The portals to Haida houses, made of the soft cedar wood that grows so abundantly in the Pacific Northwest, were also carved as totems.

The Power of the Potlatch

Potlatch is a term that may have come from a Nootka word meaning "to give." At its simplest, the potlatch was a ceremonial celebration of gift-giving among families and clans of people in the Pacific Northwest. But the potlatch served more significant purposes, both social and economic. As a social institution, the potlatch was used to establish a family's rank and position in the social hierarchy. As an economic institution, the potlatch established an understanding of wealth and its distribution among Pacific Northwestern society. Gifts were given from one group to another and back again. Artwork, food, land, blankets, copper, canoes—even slaves—were among the items offered in the potlatch.

After first contact, European goods entered the potlatch economy. Because these European goods were not locally made, yet were highly prized, only the wealthiest clans and families could afford to bestow European items among their potlatch gifts. This upset the balance of trade among the Pacific Northwestern people and caused poorer clans and families to impoverish themselves in an effort to meet the value of the potlatch gifts bestowed by wealthier clans. Missionaries complained about the materialism of the potlatch, further eroding the system. Then, in 1884, the Canadian government made potlatch illegal in an effort to prevent further economic division and displays of material excess among the Aboriginal peoples in the Pacific Northwest. This law, which effectively ruined this elaborate Aboriginal system of economics and social order, remained in force until 1951.

People of the Pacific Northwest

At the time of first contact, almost half of the Aboriginal population in Canada lived in the Pacific Northwest. Here the lush rainforests held abundant food, a mild climate, and flourishing cultures. The people of the Pacific Northwest—including the Haida, Tlingit, Kwakiutl, Nootka, Bella Coola, Coastal Salish, and others—were wealthy, culturally diverse, and spoke at least 16 distinct languages.

White traders arrived around 1700 to discover that, unlike other Aboriginal peoples, Pacific Northwestern societies believed in ownership. That meant that the land was owned outright, as were the rights to fish and hunt on the land. Payment was expected for the exchange of just about every form of goods or services.

Pacific Northwestern people often lived in huge houses made of cedar planks supported by carved and painted beams. A chief's wealth was indicated by the size and decoration of his home, which needed to be grand to support a chief's position in the social caste system. Under the chiefs in this social order were other nobles, then commoners. In many villages, slaves made up the bottom rung on the social ladder. In addition, artists and craftspeople—who created much-prized masks, totems, and other works—were supported as a subcaste by nobles. Among the Nootka, whale hunters were also socially celebrated and held apart as special citizens in their communities.

 Like the language of the Kutenai, the Haida and Tlingit languages are not related to other Aboriginal languages. Called "isolates," these languages are unique to the peoples who spoke them.

Stoney people of the Pacific Northwest and teepee at Banff in 1906.

STONEY INDIANS

The Inuit

It is believed that the ancestors of the Inuit were nomads who crossed from Siberia to Canada more than 5,000 years ago. Among Canada's Inuit are eight main tribal groups. Each of these groups speaks a dialect of Inuktitut, a language spoken across Alaska and eastern Siberia, as well as in Greenland. The Inuit were hunters and fishers. In the summer, they would travel in groups of up to a dozen, but they gathered in the winter in larger groups.

Musk oxen, waterfowl, seals, whales, and even polar bears were important to their economy, but the caribou was the most prized animal. It was a source not just of meat, but also fat for candles, hides for summer tents, bedding, and kayak skins, bones for tools, hooves for cups, and more. Although in the past Inuit travelled by dogsled, most who continue to hunt today use snowmobiles.

The Inuit had to adapt to life in a harsh Arctic wilderness. To do so, they created a number of items, many of which are also of value in less harsh climes and well known around the world today—for example, parkas, and kayaks.

Igloos

The igloo, in addition to being a symbol of the Inuit people, is a remarkable example of engineering. This winter dwelling, constructed of blocks of snow, is held together by a keystone slid into the top. After the keystone is secured, a small hole is cut into it for ventilation.

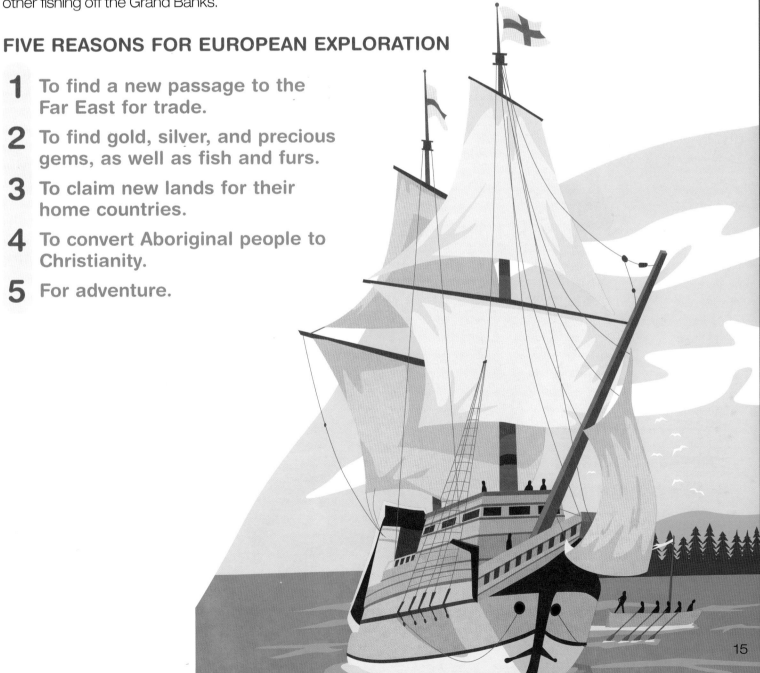

European Explorers Find a New World

In 1492, life among North America's Aboriginal peoples began to change dramatically. Christopher Columbus, an Italian explorer sailing for Spain, was hoping to find a new route to the Spice Islands near India. Thinking he had arrived, he called the people he met "Indians." Many explorers, sailing on behalf of a variety of European countries, followed Columbus to the New World. Shortly after Columbus sailed for Spain, John Cabot (Giovanni Caboto) sailed to the New World on behalf of the English Crown. Like Columbus, Cabot was seeking a westward route to the Spice Islands, although Cabot is credited with discovering Canada and opening up massive European interest in cod and other fishing off the Grand Banks.

FIVE REASONS FOR EUROPEAN EXPLORATION

1 To find a new passage to the Far East for trade.

2 To find gold, silver, and precious gems, as well as fish and furs.

3 To claim new lands for their home countries.

4 To convert Aboriginal people to Christianity.

5 For adventure.

Exploration Routes

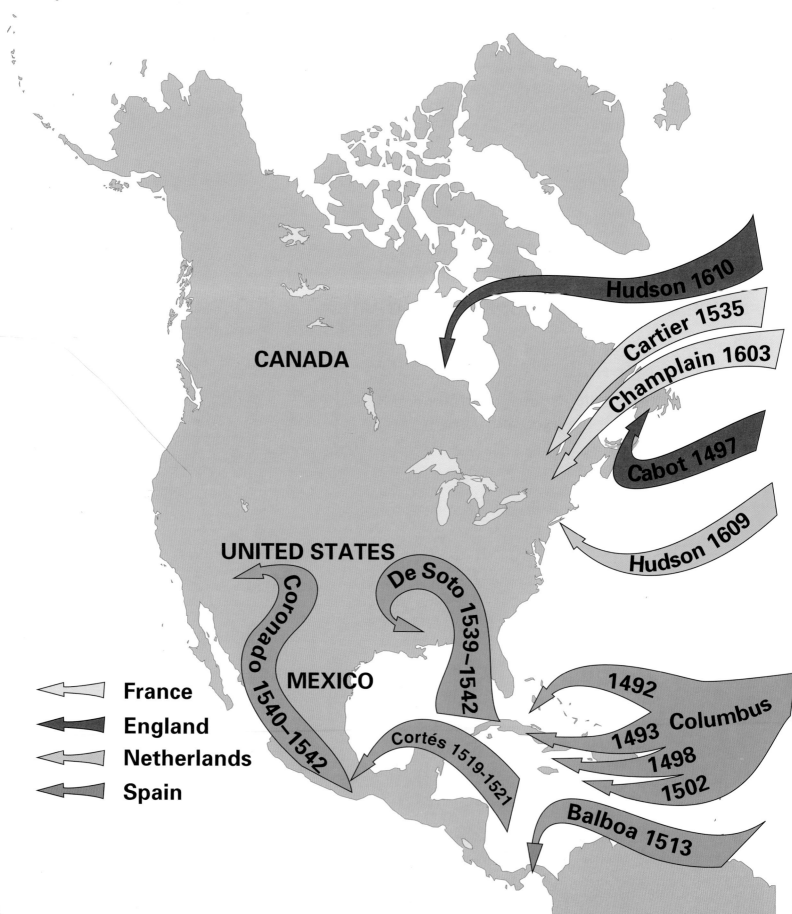

CANADA

Hudson 1610

Cartier 1535

Champlain 1603

Cabot 1497

Hudson 1609

UNITED STATES

De Soto 1539–1542

Coronado 1540–1542

MEXICO

Cortés 1519–1521

1492

1493 Columbus

1498

1502

Balboa 1513

France

England

Netherlands

Spain

SOUTH AMERICA

EARLY EUROPEAN EXPLORERS (IN CHRONOLOGICAL ORDER)

EXPLORERS	COUNTRY REPRESENTED	YEAR OF EXPLORATION	JOURNEY
Leif Ericsson	Vikings (Norway)	About 1000	Newfoundland
Bartolomeu Dias	Portugal	1487–1488	First European to round Cape of Good Hope at the southern tip of Africa
Christopher Columbus	Spain	1492 1493 1498 1502	San Salvador, Cuba, Puerto Rico, Jamaica, West Indies, Trinidad, parts of South America
John Cabot	England	1497	Greenland, Labrador, Newfoundland
Vasco da Gama	Portugal	1497–1498	First to reach India from Europe by sea
Amerigo Vespucci	Spain	1497–1502	South America and West Indies
Pedro Cabral	Portugal	1500	Sailed around Africa to India; Brazil
Ferdinand Magellan	Spain	1509–1522	First to sail around the world
Vasco de Balboa	Spain	1513	Pacific Ocean
Juan Ponce de León	Spain	1513	Florida
Hernán Cortés	Spain	1519–1521	Aztec kingdom of Mexico
Giovanni da Verrazano	France	1524	Eastern coast of North America
Pánfilo de Narváez	Spain	1528	Florida and Mexico
Francisco Pizarro	Spain	1531	Inca empire of Peru
Jacques Cartier	France	1534-1536	St. Lawrence River, Gulf of St. Lawrence
Hernando de Soto	Spain	1539–1542	Mississippi River, American Southeast
Francisco de Coronado	Spain	1540–1542	American Southwest
Juan Rodríguez Cabrillo	Spain	1542	California
Sir Francis Drake	England	1577–1580	Around the world
Samuel de Champlain	France	1603–1607	Nova Scotia, St. Lawrence River, Quebec
Henry Hudson	Netherlands England	1609 1610	Hudson River and Hudson Bay

Vinland the Good

In the 1960s, Norwegian archaeologists unearthed the remains of a Viking settlement at L'Anse aux Meadows on the northern tip of Newfoundland. The site, which could be the remains of a Viking settlement party that left Greenland in the early 1000s, contained homes, workshops, a bathhouse, kiln, and a forge. In 1978, L'Anse aux Meadows was declared a United Nations World Heritage Site. This area could be the place that the Norse called Vinland, although Viking settlements even further south (into the United States) also claim to be the Vinland of legend.

The Vikings

Europeans had visited the shores of North America even before the celebrated voyages of Christopher Columbus and his fellow explorers. These Europeans were the Vikings, Norsemen who travelled from Scandinavia (present day Norway, Sweden, and Denmark) to establish settlements in Ireland, Iceland, and Greenland before turning their boats still further west toward North America.

Around the year 1000—nearly 500 years before Columbus—Leif Ericsson left Greenland in search of "unknown lands." He sailed west and it's believed that he and his crew arrived at Baffin Island, which, according to legends, he named **Helluland**, meaning "land of flat stones." Then they headed south, probably arriving in Labrador, which they called **Markland**, "land of the woods." The Norse continued sailing south, landing in a spot they named **Vinland**, which means either "land of wine" or "land of vines."

 Snorri, a boy born in the early 1000s, is believed to be the first European child born in the New World.

Cabot, Cartier, and Champlain: England and France Make Claims

CABOT

Many historians believe that John Cabot, an Italian who sailed for King Henry VII of England, had heard from English and Portuguese fishermen about the cod-rich waters of the New World. He also had a theory. If the world really was round, then the distance between Europe and Asia should be shorter at northern latitudes than at middle latitudes. Cabot convinced the English king of his idea and left from Bristol, England, in 1497 to find a Northwest Passage (see p. 20) to the silk and spice markets of the Orient. Instead of reaching Asia, Cabot landed in North America, where he claimed a "new founde land" in the name of the English king.

John Cabot

CARTIER

Jacques Cartier left France from St. Malo on April 20, 1534, on the first of three voyages in the name of Louis XIV of France. On his first voyage, Cartier brought two ships with a combined crew of 61 men to explore the coasts of Newfoundland, Prince Edward Island, and New Brunswick, north to the Gaspé Peninsula. Cartier had hoped to find the Northwest Passage (see p. 20). Instead, he erected a large wooden cross on the Gaspé Peninsula to claim the land for King Louis.

On his second voyage in 1535, Cartier left St. Malo with three ships and 110 men, still hoping to find the Northwest Passage. He sailed down the St. Lawrence to Stadacona (present day Quebec) and on to Hochelaga, a large Iroquois village consisting of nearly 50 longhouses and more than a thousand inhabitants. Here, stopped in his progress by the Lachine rapids upstream, Cartier climbed a forested hill and planted another cross to claim Mont Royal (Montreal) for King Louis.

Cartier's third voyage in 1541 was intended less to seek the Northwest Passage than to establish a colony on the St. Lawrence and to discover treasure. Cartier proved unsuccessful at both tasks, abandoning his settlement and returning to France with pyrite (fool's gold) and "Canadian diamonds" (quartz).

Cartier may not have been successful at finding a Northwest Passage, or at unearthing treasure in the New World, but he opened the door to French claims in a land he called "Canada."

Jacques Cartier

 *Cartier thought "Canada," from the Iroquois word **kanata**, meaning "village," was a name for the entire region surrounding the St. Lawrence River. Although based on a misunderstanding, the name stuck and now describes the second-largest country in the world as "the village."*

CHAMPLAIN

Samuel de Champlain, "the Father of New France," was the first Frenchman to successfully establish a colony in North America. Following Champlain came a variety of European fur traders, adventurers, missionaries, and settlers who would forever change the face of the continent.

Champlain came to North America as an explorer, arriving in the Bay of Fundy around 1603. He helped to found the French settlements at St. Croix and Port Royal before moving down the St. Lawrence in 1608 to what is now Quebec City. Here Champlain built his colony.

 Champlain arrived at the site of Quebec City nearly 70 years after Cartier, who had described a wealthy settlement of Iroquois called the Stadacona living there. By the time Champlain arrived, the Stadacona had disappeared—perhaps because of disease (see p. 21) or intertribal warfare.

Samuel de Champlain

The Northwest Passage

The hope of a shorter route connecting Europe to the spice-rich Orient spurred many a European expedition to the New World. Cabot and Cartier (see p. 18–19) were among the many who ran into the North American continent in their effort to find a Northwest Passage. Many others would continue the quest over the centuries following first contact on North American shores.

Henry Hudson, in the ship *Discovery*, sailed from England in 1610 with a crew of 22. Although he failed to find the Northwest Passage, he did navigate a new sea route into the interior of present-day Canada and into the large inland bay that bears his name.

Expeditions to find the Northwest Passage continued in the centuries that followed, usually resulting in death and disaster. Sir John Franklin set sail in 1845 with 129 men and disappeared into the icy north. In an effort to rescue Franklin's mission, Robert McClure is believed by some historians to have discovered a possible route. Yet it was not until 1906 that Roald Amundsen sailed a successful expedition through the icy waters of the Arctic Ocean, navigating a Northwest Passage that no longer was practical or necessary.

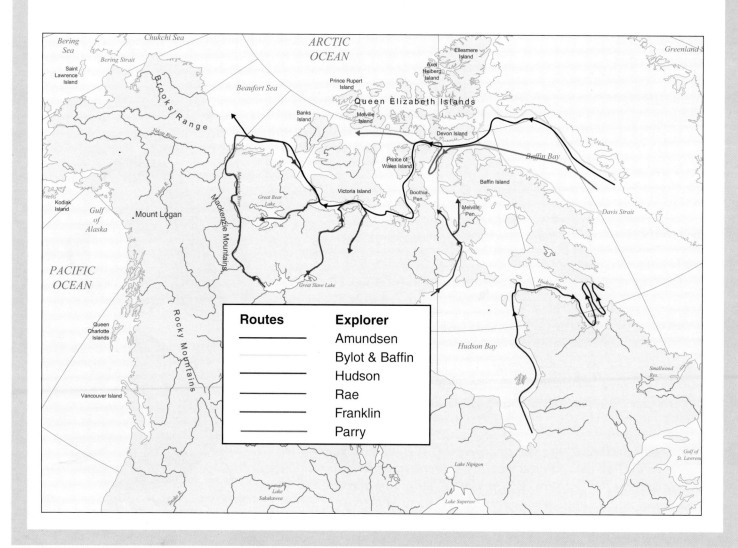

Cod

Known as "the beef of the sea," cod was a tasty source of protein that was easy to cure and store. This made it a valuable commodity to many Europeans. Cod was abundant on the shores of the Grand Banks. It was so abundant, in fact, that by the late 1600s, tens of thousands of European fishermen swarmed the waters off Newfoundland to haul in the precious catch for king and commerce.

Trading posts and temporary settlements of Basques, Portuguese, and Dutch, as well as English, French, and Spaniards, teemed Newfoundland's shores for the seasonal catch. After preserving the cod in salt and packing the fish in ships' holds, the fishermen would return to Europe to trade the salt cod in European markets. They would come back each summer to fish the Grand Banks waters for the precious commodity.

Fishing on the Grand Banks boomed across the centuries until the 1990s. The once abundant cod of Newfoundland had at last been overfished and the stocks almost depleted.

Old World Diseases in a New World

Conflicts between Aboriginal peoples and European explorers were often deadly affairs, but an unseen killer would prove as dangerous as white men's guns. The unseen killer was disease—epidemics of such illnesses as measles, smallpox, and the common cold, to name a few. Entire populations of Aboriginal peoples, who had never encountered these infections and so had no immunity to them, were accidentally wiped out by European disease. Some may have been intentionally harmed. Historical records suggest that smallpox-infested blankets were distributed among Aboriginal peoples in an effort to weaken certain tribes or even to wipe them out.

Colonies and Conflicts: New France and the English Conquest

 Acadia, or in French, Acadie, is believed to come from the Mi'kmaq word meaning "camp" or "village." It was one of France's first Canadian colonies, but control over the area went back and forth between the French and the British several times. Eventually Acadia fell to Britain, and the Acadians were forcibly deported to other parts of North America.

By 1600, Canada supported a thriving international scene of merchant fishermen and adventurers representing several European nations. But none of the European communities were year-round settlements—that is, until Samuel de Champlain set his sights on the St. Lawrence. England kept a close watch on the French adventurers in northern North America and made its own claims to what are now Canadian lands. What's more, waves of European missionaries came to stake a claim for Christianity. In the process, traditional alliances and rivalries among Aboriginal peoples shifted, creating a whole new political and economic landscape in early Canada.

By 1700, the French, already exhausted by a decades-long war with the Iroquois, were plunged headlong into a series of wars against England. Unlike their wars of the past, these new wars were fought in both Europe and North America.

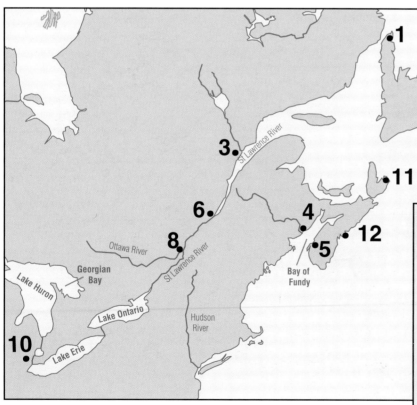

Early European Settlements

1. L'Anse aux Meadows—Norse: around 1000s
2. St. John's—Britain: 1583
3. Tadoussac—France: around 1600
4. St. Croix Island—France: 1604
5. Port Royal—France: 1605
6. Quebec—France: 1608
7. Cupids—Britain: 1610
8. Montreal—France: 1642
9. Placentia—France: 1624
10. Detroit—France: 1701
11. Louisbourg—France: 1713
12. Halifax—Britain: 1749

Champlain and the Iroquois

Samuel de Champlain's settlement at Quebec—taken from the Algonquian word *quebecq*, meaning "where the river narrows"—was established upriver from a Basque fishing settlement at Tadoussac. (The Basques came there from their homeland in the Pyrenees Mountain region that separates France and Spain.) Champlain avoided conflict with the Basques. However, he made himself an enemy of the Mohawk by repeatedly raiding their holdings. The Mohawk, influential members of the League of Five Nations (see p. 8), called their Iroquois allies into years of ongoing warfare. However, Champlain moved north and formed an alliance with a separate Iroquoian group, the Hurons. The Hurons did not consider themselves to be allied with the other Iroquoians at the time, and were interested in a fruitful trading relationship with the French.

Samuel de Champlain trading with Aboriginal people, early 17th century. Oil on board painting by C. W. Jefferys.

The Hudson's Bay Company, founded in 1670, is still in operation today, making it the oldest ongoing business in the world.

The original **coureur de bois** *was Étienne Brûlé. He had lived among the Huron for years prior to Champlain's arrival at Quebec. Brûlé served as an interpreter for Champlain and helped him negotiate agreements for the Aboriginal-French fur trade.*

From Fishing to the Fur Trade

Champlain's settlement at Quebec, and his alliance with the Huron, opened up a new industry in the New World: the fur trade. To establish the trade, Champlain sent young men to live in the woods among the Huron and other Aboriginal allies, to learn their customs and languages. These men were called **coureurs de bois**, French for "runners of the woods."

For the most part, the French controlled the fur trade until 1670, when the English founded the Hudson's Bay Company. The Hudson's Bay Company followed the newly explored northern route to the Canadian inland, which led them north of the St. Lawrence River. It also sandwiched the French between English holdings in the north (Hudson's Bay Company) and the south (the thirteen American colonies).

A Hudson's Bay Company fort

Habitants

Champlain, while establishing the fur trade, also encouraged settlement. Led by Louis Hébert, the **habitants** cleared the land and planted crops in New France. This began a slow process that shifted the focus of French interests from the fur trade to agriculture in the New World.

Food for the Soul:
The Récollets and the Jesuits

While Louis Hébert and the *habitants* (see above) grew food for New France stomachs, two groups of missionaries joined the traders and settlers of New France to feed Aboriginal and European souls: the Récollets and the Jesuits.

Arriving in 1615, the Récollet missionaries tried to introduce Christianity to the Algonquian people, but made little headway. The Jesuits, who arrived ten years later, were somewhat more successful. Like the *coureurs de bois*, the Jesuits chose to live among the Aboriginal peoples (especially among the Huron), learning their customs and languages. Although accepted by the Huron at first, the Jesuits came to be feared. Unintentionally, they had brought with them a smallpox epidemic that wiped out nearly half the Huron population. What's more, their gospel divided the Huron nation into Christian and unconverted factions, a social division that set brother against brother.

The Huron were greatly weakened by disease and the religious division in their traditional social structure. Constant military conflicts had led to famine. This made them vulnerable to attack. In 1648, the Huron were overrun by the Iroquois (see p. 23). By 1649, the Jesuits abandoned their mission at Sainte-Marie-Among-the-Hurons and retreated to Quebec with some 600 Huron refugees.

Home-grown Feudalism: The Seigneurial System

In the late 1620s, an Old World feudal system was founded in the New World. Called the seigneurial system, it granted land titles to individuals and institutions deemed deserving by the French Crown. These "deserving" people, or *seigneurs*, were usually French nobles, soldiers, or religious leaders, but also included wealthy and well-connected common people. *Seigneurs* were expected to live on and develop the lands granted to them. To do so, the *seigneurs* brought in labourers—the *habitants*—to clear fields, build manor houses, and create farms. In exchange, the *habitants* were allowed to lease lands from the *seigneur* with the right to pass the lease on to their children as if it were their personal property. From the collaboration of *seigneurs* and *habitants* emerged a new nationality, one French in tradition but North American in spirit—the *Canadien*.

The Iroquois Wars (1684–1701)

As they ventured west into Iroquois fur-trading territory around Lake Ontario, the French once again clashed with the Iroquois. Here the Iroquois Confederacy (see p. 8) had established itself as a powerful middleman in the fur trade—a middleman armed with English guns obtained from colonists in English-held New York. A series of clashes with the Iroquois weakened the French stronghold over the next two decades:

1684	The French attempt a raid on Iroquois holdings deep within Iroquois Confederacy lands.
1687	Iroquois tribesmen meet with French delegates to negotiate a ceasefire but are taken captive and sent to France as slaves.
1689	After enduring five years of French assaults on Iroquois lands, the Iroquois counterattack at the French settlement of Lachine, killing more than 20 settlers and taking another 50 or more captive.
1689–1700	Iroquois Confederacy wages all-out war against New France.
1701	A peace treaty signals the end of warfare between the *Canadiens* and the Iroquois Confederacy.

The Fur Wars (1613–1763)

The French found themselves fighting more than the Iroquois in New France. Starting around 1613, a variety of English-French struggles were played out in North America, as well as in Europe:

1629–33	The English capture Quebec and take Champlain prisoner.
1654–70	The French colony of Acadia falls under English rule.
1670s–1680s	Acadians establish informal local governments despite English authority.
1686	French raid Hudson's Bay Company posts in James Bay as part of ongoing "fur war" in North America.
1689–97	King William's War (in Europe, War of the League of Augsburg). English temporarily recapture Acadia but fail to capture Quebec. French capture Hudson's Bay Company forts and raid English settlements in Newfoundland.

1702–1713	Queen Anne's War (in Europe, War of the Spanish Succession). British capture Acadia once and for all. Port Royal is renamed Port Annapolis. The Treaty of Utrecht gives French claims in the Hudson Bay area, Acadia, and Newfoundland to England.
1713–1740	Era of peace between England and France. France establishes new settlement at Louisbourg.
1744–48	King George's War (in Europe, War of Austrian Succession, 1739–48). Louisbourg is captured (1745), but is returned by treaty. British establish Halifax.
1755–62	Acadians deported.
1756–63	Seven Years War in Europe (in North America, the French and Indian War, 1754-63).

With the Treaty of Paris (see p. 29), France gave up control of New France and its settlements in the Maritimes (see Chronology of the Seven Years War, p. 28–29).

CAUSES OF THE FUR WARS

1 Tensions between France and England in Europe spilled over into the New World.

2 British colonists wanted to take over French lands to make money in the fur trade.

3 French expansion into western territories as part of their effort to increase their fur trade, while cutting off English routes, deepened tensions between The League of Five Nations (see p. 8) and the French. This led to escalated attacks on French settlements by member nations of the Iroquois Confederacy.

Still Searching for China: La Salle and the Mississippi

In 1682, René-Robert Cavelier, Sieur de La Salle, set off on a journey that led him from his seigneurial manor (see p. 26) in New France, west along the Great Lakes, then south to the Mississippi River—all the way to its delta. The territory he covered, named Louisiana for the French king, made La Salle one of France's most celebrated explorers. But he, like so many before him, was unsuccessful in finding a "western sea" and a new route to China.

Beavers were trapped for their fur.

In 1755, the population of New France totalled no more than 60,000 people. Compare that to the 1.2 million British subjects living in Britain's thirteen American colonies!

The Seven Years War

In North America, shooting in the Seven Years War started two years before war was actually declared in Europe. In 1753, George Washington delivered a letter to Fort Duquesne, a French outpost in the Ohio River Valley. The letter, from the Virginia Royal Governor, demanded that the French leave the area. The French didn't budge. Washington, with 150 armed troops, returned in 1754. He and his men ambushed a *Canadien* patrol and killed 10 men before they withdrew, taking 21 prisoners.

By 1755, British governors from the American colonies met at Alexandria, Virginia, to organize another assault. Their plan was to attack four French strongholds: Fort Duquesne, Niagara, Lake Champlain, and Acadia. Only the assault on Acadia was successful.

CHRONOLOGY OF THE SEVEN YEARS WAR

1756   French general Montcalm's victory at Fort Oswego gives France control of the Great Lakes.

1757   Montcalm, aided by Aboriginal allies, captures Fort William Henry in upper New York.

1758   Montcalm prevents a British invasion at Fort Carillon. Louisbourg falls to the British under General Amherst.

Before the Treaty of Paris

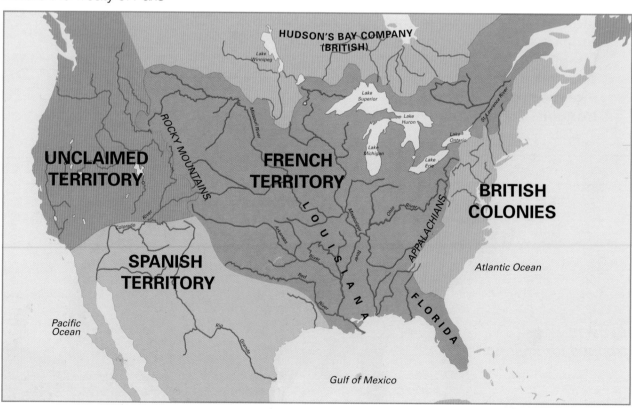

1759 In the Battle for Quebec, the French, outnumbered three to one, hold off British regulars for months before being defeated on the Plains of Abraham on September 13. Both General Montcalm and Britain's General Wolfe are killed.

1760 In the Battle of Sainte-Foy, the French attempt to recapture Quebec, but the British hold on to the city.

RESULTS OF THE SEVEN YEARS WAR: THE TREATY OF PARIS (1763)

1 France lost most of its power in North America.

2 Spain took over New Orleans and all the French territory west of the Mississippi River.

3 Britain took over Canada and all the French territory east of the Mississippi, except New Orleans.

4 Britain placed all its colonies under strict control and began taxing them to help pay for the cost of the war.

After the Treaty of Paris (1763)

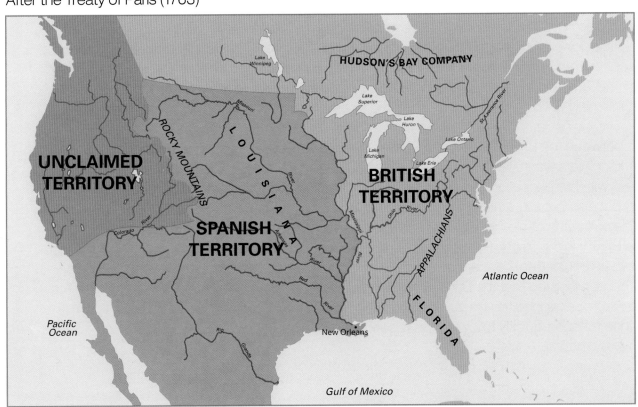

The Pontiac Rebellion (1763–1765)

Following the Treaty of Paris in 1763, the British struggled to establish control over Quebec, the newly named province, which was made up of the former lands of New France. In addition to policy regarding the *Canadiens* (see p. 26), the British had established a handful of peace treaties with some of the Aboriginal peoples. However, when the British took up their claim to former French trading areas, they stirred up the enmity of the Aboriginal peoples, including the Seneca, a member of the Iroquois Confederacy (see p. 8). The British had previously been allied with the Seneca against the French. As English settlers moved into Seneca lands, the presumed friendships failed.

An Aboriginal medicine man, the "Delaware Prophet," called for Aboriginal peoples to return to their roots and reject trade and commerce with Europeans of all nationalities. Pontiac, an Ottawa chief, heard the prophet's message and created an alliance among the Ottawa, Ojibwa, Potawatomi, and Seneca to resist British settlement and maintain their claim to the forests, mountains, lakes, and woodlands of Quebec.

The conflict between the British and Pontiac's allies lasted two years. In that time, more than 2,000 settlers and 400 soldiers were killed. The allied Aboriginal resistance also captured all the British forts west of Niagara, with the exception of the fort at Detroit. In all, the rebellion cost the British dearly, not only in people, but also in pride. It also ignited British hatred of Aboriginal people.

Following many months of bloodshed, Pontiac, representing the Aboriginal alliance, signed a peace treaty with the British. In the treaty, Pontiac insisted that Aboriginal peoples would never recognize British subjects as owners of Quebec's lands. Instead, they would be viewed as tenants on Aboriginal lands. Furthermore, Pontiac insisted that the British limit their occupation to trading posts and not settle on the land. The British agreed, signed the treaty, and promptly went back on their word. Meanwhile, the Aboriginal alliance fell apart quickly following the rebellion, and Chief Pontiac was later killed by an assassin from a rival nation.

Chapter 5 Road to Canada

The Quebec Act (1774)

In 1763, Britain issued a Royal Proclamation. The proclamation gave Protestant landowners in Canada the right to elect an assembly to govern its newly created province of Quebec. This policy was aimed at controlling Catholic French-Canadians who had come under British rule as a result of the Seven Years War (see p. 28–29). Under the terms of the proclamation, for example, Roman Catholics (often French) were barred from serving as representatives. The policy was also meant to please the English merchants who had established them-selves in French Canada, especially in Quebec City and Montreal. The Royal Proclamation failed due to its many flaws and was embraced by neither the *Canadiens* nor the English settlers. The British acknowledged the shortcomings of the Proclamation and replaced it in 1774 with the Quebec Act. Overall, the Act created a unique mix of French and Canadian traditions of law and religion. It also set off a storm of protest in the American colonies and among Aboriginal people, who saw the terms of the Act as an effort to limit free trade and to usurp land rights understood to be held by Aboriginal peoples.

MAJOR TERMS OF THE QUEBEC ACT

1 The Royal Governor appointed a council to administer Quebec. There would be no elected assembly, and *Canadiens* could be among those appointed to the council.

2 French civil law was reinstated in matters of property ownership, and the seigneurial system was recognized. Criminal law followed British law.

3 The Roman Catholic Church retained some of the rights it held under French law—rights that were not allowed the Catholic Church in England.

4 The boundaries of Quebec were redrawn to include the fur trading regions of the Great Lakes, westward to the Mississippi.

Historians believe that nearly half of Benedict Arnold's siege force died from starvation, disease, cold, and exhaustion during the march from Montreal to Quebec in November and December, 1775.

The American Revolution (1775–1783)

In 1775, after cutting their ties to Britain, the Continental Congress of the American rebels voted to invade Canada. They wanted to set Canada free from British rule and to prevent Britain from using Canada as a military base in a war against the 13 American colonies.

By September 1775, rebel forces had launched a siege against Montreal. By November, the rebel army took the city and turned toward Quebec. Here the invasion failed when American forces under Benedict Arnold arrived fatigued and without sufficient provisions to mount a lengthy siege. After a prolonged struggle, the Americans withdrew from Canada, and the Treaty of Paris, 1783, formally recognized the United States of America as a country.

RESULTS OF THE AMERICAN REVOLUTION: THE TREATY OF PARIS, 1783

1 Britain lost the 13 American colonies, which became an independent nation called the United States of America. Britain formally recognized the new nation.

2 Britain gave the United States all lands east of the Mississippi River, north to Canada, and south to Florida. The border with Canada was drawn at the Great Lakes.

3 All British control of United States trade was lifted. The United States was free to enter trade agreements on its own.

4 Britain gave Aboriginal land rights—which weren't its to offer—as peace offerings to the United States. In turn, the United States offered to pay Loyalists, who were forced to leave the colonies, for their land.

The Constitutional Act, 1791

The Constitutional Act, 1791 established a structure of government that can be seen today in the framework of the Canadian federal system (see p. 43). Under the Act:

1 The province of Quebec was divided into Upper Canada (roughly the modern province of Ontario) and Lower Canada (modern Quebec) along the Ottawa River. Upper Canada was primarily English, and Lower Canada was mostly French.

2 The colonial government consisted of a governor who represented British authority.

3 Under the governor was the governor's appointed council.

4 Under the council was an elected assembly that represented male landowners.

The Constitutional Act, 1791

The War of 1812 (1812–1814)

The War of 1812 has been called "Canada's War of Independence." Although it was a war declared by the United States against Britain, it resulted in Canada remaining independent of the United States.

CAUSES OF THE WAR OF 1812

1 Because Britain was at war with France, it tried to prevent other nations from trading with France. France was one of the United States' biggest trade partners, so the British were capturing American ships that they suspected were bound for France.

2 Britain would also board foreign ships, hoping to catch British citizens who could be pressed into military service against the French. The Americans considered these boardings attacks on their independence. At one point an American ship was actually fired upon; two men were killed.

3 The United States believed that the British were arming Aboriginal peoples and encouraging them to attack settlers in the Northwest Territory, the land north of the Ohio River between the established United States and the Mississippi River.

4 After buying land from France (known as the Louisiana Purchase), the United States wanted to take Canada from Britain and Florida from Spain and to acquire all the land in North America under its flag. Since Britain was busy fighting the French in Europe, the United States believed that Canada would be relatively undefended and vulnerable to attack.

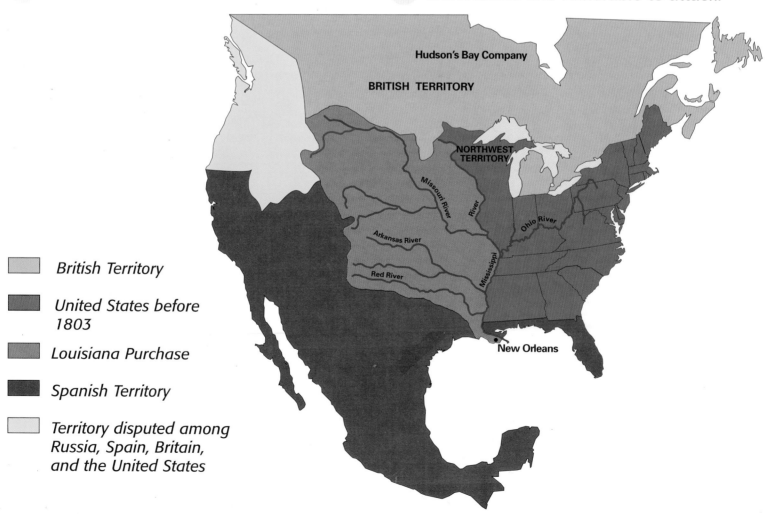

British Territory

United States before 1803

Louisiana Purchase

Spanish Territory

Territory disputed among Russia, Spain, Britain, and the United States

RESULTS OF THE WAR OF 1812

1 Britain and the United States established and recognized boundaries in the Northwest Territory.

2 The Treaty of Ghent set the American-Canadian border along pre-war lines, but gave the United States freedom to settle western lands at will, despite British treaties reserving these lands for Aboriginal peoples.

3 The Rush-Bagot Agreement, finalized in 1817, limited U.S. and Canada naval armaments along the Great Lakes.

4 An agreement enacted at the Convention of 1818 set the boundary between the United States and Canada at the 49th parallel from the Lake of the Woods (west of Lake Superior) to the Rocky Mountains. The lands west of the Rockies were left open for joint exploration.

5 British Loyalists from the United States left that politically divided nation to live among other British subjects in Canada. Their contributions would make a tremendous impact on the politics and economy of Canada in the years to follow, especially in Ontario and the western provinces.

The Rush-Bagot Agreement of 1817 began the development of "the longest undefended border in the world," the border that still exists between the United States and Canada.

Some Events of the War of 1812

1812 On June 18, the United States declares war on Britain.

On July 12, Americans launch their invasion, sending a force of 2,500 from Detroit into Upper Canada. Repelled at Fort Michilimackinac (at Mackinac Island in present-day northern Michigan), the Americans retreat to Detroit, which falls to the British under General Brock and their Shawnee allies.

At the battle of Queenston Heights, the British hold off the Americans, but at a great cost, including the death of General Brock.

In November, U.S. troops control Lake Ontario but are defeated in their efforts to capture York (present-day Toronto). The United States makes three attempts to invade Canada, but all end in failure.

1813 Americans take control of the Great Lakes and capture York. They loot the city and burn many of the government buildings.

Americans make a two-pronged attack on Montreal, south from New York and east from the Great Lakes. The first invasion force is defeated by Canadian and Mohawk allies at the Battle of Châteauguay. The second is repelled at Crysler's Farm by Canadian and British troops.

1814 Americans capture Fort Erie.

In retaliation for the burning of York, the British burn Washington, D.C., including the White House.

The Treaty of Ghent is signed, agreeing to peace between Britain and the United States.

1815 News of the Treaty of Ghent doesn't reach North America in time to prevent British troops from attempting an invasion of the United States at New Orleans. The British are repelled.

General Brock and Chief Tecumseh

Isaac Brock, a British general and Governor of Upper Canada, was charged with defending his province from U.S. attack during the War of 1812. Many Americans had settled in Upper Canada and Brock was concerned about their loyalty.

Brock proved to be an inspirational leader, as well as a brilliant strategist. He needed more manpower, so Brock turned to Aboriginal allies to bolster his troops. Stepping in under the leadership of Shawnee chief Tecumseh was an Aboriginal alliance representing more than a dozen groups, including the Shawnee, Ottawa, Delaware, Miami, Wyandot, Chippewa, Fox, Potawatomi, Dakota, Kickapoo, Sauk, and Winnebago.

Together, Brock and Tecumseh shared two goals:

1. Stop American expansion into Upper Canada, and
2. Challenge U.S. claims to interior lands west of the Ohio River, stretching from the Great Lakes to Florida.

In the end, the poorly organized U.S. forces couldn't outmaneouvre the combined mind- and manpower mustered by Isaac Brock and Chief Tecumseh, who, together, are credited with saving Upper Canada from U.S. invasion.

The Rebellions of 1837

By 1837, British North America was made up of Upper Canada (Ontario), Lower Canada (Quebec), New Brunswick, Nova Scotia, and Prince Edward Island. Although the War of 1812 had stopped U.S. efforts to annex Canada, two issues came to a head in Britain's "loyal" colonies. These issues—the Family Compact and French assimilation—were complex, but both led to a common goal: to gain local, elected control of government from appointed British governors.

In Upper Canada, the issue was the Family Compact. The Family Compact was the name given to the loyalist ruling faction of the local government that supported anti-American attitudes, English customs and culture, and British royal government. Moderate reformers in the province had little effect in changing attitudes among these government representatives, but reform ultimately was led by the journalist William Lyon Mackenzie.

The demand for expanded individual rights and freedoms in Upper Canada escalated at Montgomery's Tavern in Toronto. Calling for the liberation of Canada, Mackenzie declared himself President of Canada and led a band of 600 armed men from the tavern down Yonge Street. Mackenzie was quickly defeated by a volunteer force sent out by the governor. However, his rebellion planted seeds of sympathy for self-government even in the loyalist soil of Upper Canada. Over the years, Mackenzie encouraged reform of the Family Compact and struggled to gain momentum for a constitutional movement in Canada, one that represented all Canadian people—not just the British elites.

 First elected to the assembly in 1828, William Lyon Mackenzie was expelled immediately from office by the ruling elite. He was re-elected and expelled three more times before becoming the first mayor of Toronto in 1834.

William Lyon Mackenzie

The reformers in both Upper and Lower Canada sought "responsible government," a system of self-government in which the governor is responsible (that is, he must answer to) a legislature of elected, rather than appointed, representatives.

In Lower Canada, the issue was French assimilation. The seigneurial estates (see p. 26) by this point had come into the control of English-speaking lords, who aligned themselves with wealthy merchant families in Montreal. They supported the government as outlined in the Constitutional Act, 1791 (see p. 33), and were part of the so-called **Château Clique** that ruled Lower Canada. Against them stood the **Parti Patriote**, who authored the **92 Resolutions** in 1834. The *Parti Patriote* represented the majority of people and held the most representatives in the elected assembly. They were upset by the amount of power that the English and the Church held over their lives. The *Parti Patriote*'s 92 Resolutions demanded that the elected assembly have more control over the government by requiring that the Royal Governor select his council from elected representatives. Britain said "no" to all 92 of the resolutions, and battle lines were drawn. Joining the *Patriotes* were anti-British Vermonters and New Yorkers. Soon, the *Patriotes*, led by Louis-Joseph Papineau, were holding rallics and threatening to take up arms. The British tried to quell the rising rebellion, but the *Patriotes* would not back down. In all, nearly 300 French Canadians died in six battles fought between 1837 and 1839.

Francis Bond Head

Francis Bond Head, appointed Lieutenant Governor of Upper Canada in 1836, is credited by many historians with putting down William Lyon Mackenzie and his rebellion (see p. 37). He is also known for his ill-considered policies regarding Aboriginal people. For example, Bond Head promised the Ojibwa protected lands in exchange for 1.5 million acres of land in northern Ontario. Bond Head's policies represented an effort to force a separation between European and Aboriginal people. However, when the "protected" lands were ultimately offered—on the barren Manitoulin Island— Aboriginal people were outraged at having been duped in a land grabbing scheme. In the end, very few Aboriginal people took up the governor's Manitoulin offer.

The Act of Union (1841)

Enacted on February 10, 1841, the Act of Union was intended to answer the concerns raised in the Rebellions of 1837. While it did not provide for "responsible government," it did serve as some compromise between the prevailing systems and the demands made by reformers.

TERMS OF THE ACT OF UNION

1 Upper and Lower Canada were to be united under one government, called the Province of Canada, and would be divided into Canada West (mainly English-speaking) and Canada East (mainly French-speaking).

2 The assembly would have the same number of representatives from Canada West and Canada East, despite the fact that Canada East had a larger population.

3 Canada West's large debt would be pooled with Canada East's smaller one to bail out the virtually bankrupt region.

4 English would be the only official language of government.

RESULTS OF THE ACT OF UNION

The Act of Union was mostly unsuccessful in addressing the growing pains of Britain's North American colonies, and over the following 15 years, many of its clauses were repealed. However, the combined province of Canada East and West created some important legislation and public policies:

1 Formal school systems—in both French and English—were established.

2 Britain, by refusing to continue favoured trade policies to its colonies, opened Canada to developing its own trade agreements (for instance, the 1854 Reciprocity Treaty with the United States).

3 The seigneurial system was abolished (1854).

4 The construction of railways was encouraged, including the Grand Trunk Railway that linked Quebec City to Portland, Maine, in the United States.

Timeline Toward Responsible Government

Responsible Government was won in the provinces:

1848 Nova Scotia
Province of Canada (Ontario and Quebec)

1851 Prince Edward Island

1854 New Brunswick

Fraser River Gold Rush! The Birth of British Columbia

In 1849, the island of Vancouver was made a Crown colony. For the next ten years, the colony's economy was based primarily on the fur trade, although small coal mining communities were prospering. Then, in 1858, gold was discovered on the Fraser River.

Within weeks, the population of Victoria rose from around 450 citizens to nearly 5,000 gold-hungry adventurers. Although most of the gold miners simply passed through on their way to the Fraser and the gold fields, many stayed and settled in the town. By 1858, a second Crown colony was established on the mainland, called British Columbia.

Boundary Issues

The expansionist goals of the United States were keenly felt by British North Americans in the War of 1812 (see p. 34). Although Britain and the United States would avoid declared war in the following years, tensions over national expansion and boundaries nevertheless remained high. These tensions resulted in a series of treaties and agreements, defining large sections of boundaries separating the British colonies in Canada from the United States. However, several areas remained in dispute, among them the boundaries separating Maine and New Brunswick, and those separating Oregon Territory settlements from Hudson's Bay Company lands west of the Rocky Mountains.

The Aroostook War (1839–1842) erupted over land rights separating the newly formed U.S. state of Maine and the colony of New Brunswick. Resolved in the Webster-Ashburton Treaty, the Maine-New Brunswick boundary defined New Brunswick's boundary along a crucial strip of land at the tip of Maine and the south shore of the St. Lawrence River, linking New Brunswick to Canada East.

The Convention of 1818 had failed to define clear boundaries in the lands west of the Rockies. Here, U.S. and British fur trade enterprises, as well as American settlers moving north through the Oregon Territory, vied for claim to the land with the Hudson's Bay Company (see p. 24).

Tensions increased dramatically in 1844 when U.S. president James Polk adopted a campaign to establish American holdings all the way up the Pacific Coast. But Polk's plan would have cut off British North America from any claim along the Pacific Ocean. Instead, Britain suggested a border drawn at the 45th parallel, along the Columbia River. Ultimately, in the Oregon Boundary Settlement of 1846, the northern border was recognized to follow the 49th parallel, straight through the Rockies to the western shore of Lake Superior. In the settlement, the United States agreed that Vancouver Island would remain British.

Canadian Confederation

John A. Macdonald

 In 1864, John A. Macdonald ended the stalemate in the Province of Canada's parliament. He crossed party lines to join in the Great Coalition, which called for:

1. *A federation of all provinces and territories of British North America.*

2. *The Canadian government to be based on the principle of representation by population.*

3. *Canadians to expand their interests into the northwest to hold off U.S. expansion into the Pacific.*

KEYS TO CONFEDERATION

1 A change in British attitudes: Britain had begun to regard its colonies as expensive. Britain began to promote trade and profit over military strength and land monopolies.

2 Canadians feared the United States might attack them because of British sympathies to the Confederate States in the American Civil War. Also, U.S.-Canada trade was threatened when the United States failed to renew the Treaty of Reciprocity.

3 The railway made travel across vast distances possible and could connect far-removed provinces one to the other. Consequently, it served as an incentive for other provinces, especially British Columbia, to join Confederation. The cost to build it was higher than any one province could bear, however, so Confederation would also provide the shared means to make the railway scheme possible.

4 Canadians were unhappy with the political deadlock in the Province of Canada. This was created by having equal numbers of representatives in government from Canada West and Canada East, despite the considerable differences in population. A movement to base representation on population became part of the Confederation movement.

The Charlottetown and Quebec Conferences

From September 1–9, 1864, a conference was held at Charlottetown, Prince Edward Island, in an effort by "Coalition" Canadians to persuade the Atlantic provinces to join the Confederation movement. The Atlantic delegates, previously uninterested in such a move, agreed to meet again in Quebec to work out a plan for union.

The Conference convened again in Quebec from October 10–27, 1864. Here 72 resolutions were drafted and revised in an effort to create a plan for Confederation.

A FEDERAL SYSTEM

Delegates agreed that Canadian Confederation should be based on a federal system, with two levels of government:

1 A provincial government, responsible for roads, civil law, property rights, education, natural resources, and so on.

2 A federal government, responsible for money and currency systems, a military, criminal law, trade, maintenance of coastlands and waterways, and so on.

At the federal level, government would be divided into two levels: a Senate, or Upper House, consisting of appointed members; and a House of Commons, or Lower House, elected by Canadian voters.

RESULTS OF THE QUEBEC CONFERENCE

1 Newfoundland and Prince Edward Island voted against Confederation.

2 The Province of Canada voted in favour.

3 New Brunswick initially voted against but, in 1866, voted for it.

4 Nova Scotia didn't vote but adopted Confederation in 1867.

Provincial and Territorial Timeline: Joining Confederation

New Brunswick	1867
Nova Scotia	1867
Ontario	1867
Quebec	1867
Manitoba	1870
Northwest Territories	1870
British Columbia	1871
Prince Edward Island	1873
Yukon Territory	1898
Alberta	1905
Saskatchewan	1905
Newfoundland and Labrador	1949
Nunavut	1999

Following enactment of the British North America Act, Canada became known as the "Dominion of Canada," inspired by the words of Psalm 72, verse 8, in the Bible, which reads: **He shall have dominion from sea to sea.**

The British North America Act (1867)

On March 29, 1867, Queen Victoria signed into law the British North America Act (BNA Act), based on the resolutions outlined at the Charlottetown and Quebec Conferences (see p. 43). By July 1, 1867, the BNA Act was enacted and Canada was born. The original four members of Canadian Confederation were:

1 Nova Scotia
2 New Brunswick
3 Quebec
4 Ontario

The BNA Act did not grant full independence to Canada. Canadians were still subjects of the British Empire, with the Queen recognized as official Head of State. But the Act allowed for far greater self-government for Canadian citizens.

Fathers of Confederation

Thirty-six delegates attended the Confederation conferences at Charlottetown and Quebec City. Among these men, two became prime ministers, ten lieutenant-governors, nine provincial ministers, and twelve cabinet members. Following is a list of the Fathers of Confederation and the areas they represented:

Adams G. Archibald, Nova Scotia

George Brown, Canada West

Alexander Campbell, Canada West

Frederick B. T. Carter, Newfoundland

Georges-Étienne Cartier, Canada East

Edward Barron Chandler, New Brunswick

Jean-Charles Chapais, Canada East

James Cockburn, Canada West

George Coles, Prince Edward Island

Robert Barry Dickey, Nova Scotia

Charles Fisher, New Brunswick

Alexander T. Galt, Canada East

John Hamilton Gray, New Brunswick

John Hamilton Gray, Prince Edward Island

Thomas Heath Haviland, Prince Edward Island

William A. Henry, Nova Scotia

William P. Howland, Canada West

John Mercer Johnson, New Brunswick

Hector-Louis Langevin, Canada East

Andrew A. Macdonald, Prince Edward Island

John A. Macdonald, Canada West

Jonathan McCully, Nova Scotia

William McDougall, Manitoba

Thomas D'Arcy McGee, Canada East

Peter Mitchell, New Brunswick

Oliver Mowat, Canada West

Edward Palmer, Prince Edward Island

William H. Pope, Prince Edward Island

John W. Ritchie, Nova Scotia

Ambrose Shea, Newfoundland

William Henry Steeves, New Brunswick

Étienne-Paschal Taché, Canada East

Samuel L. Tilley, New Brunswick

Charles Tupper, Nova Scotia

Edward Whelan, Prince Edward Island

Robert Duncan Wilmot, New Brunswick

Growing Pains (1867–1918)

Chapter 6

In 1870, the Hudson's Bay Company agreed to sell the Northwest Territories to Canada for $1.5 million. The purchase ensured the realization of the Fathers of Confederation's dream of a Canada extending from "sea to shining sea." However, the deal also ignored Hudson's Bay Company agreements with Aboriginal peoples and with the Métis, a people of mixed Aboriginal and European background who lived on the Red River frontier near present-day Winnipeg. Although no one from the Hudson's Bay Company asked the Métis or Aboriginal peoples for their views on the sale, the people decided to speak up on their own. The seeds of more rebellions were planted.

The Numbered Treaties

Under the British North America Act, the Canadian government took over responsibility from Britain for Aboriginal lands and treaties, as well as for the protection and well-being of Aboriginal peoples. Because existing treaties covered little of the land in western Canada, the government wanted to secure land rights for its own use and keep Aboriginal claims unspecified and difficult to enforce. Between 1871 and 1921, a total of 11 treaties were made:

1 The first seven treaties were signed between 1871 and 1877.

2 These treaties provided for rights of way for Canadian railways.

3 Most of the numbered treaties provided a payment on signature, plus promises to provide schools and other resources to Aboriginal peoples.

Many Aboriginal peoples agreed to the treaties because they were poor and saw the treaty payments as a way to lift them out of poverty. Others considered them a threat to their way of life and tried to prohibit their leaders from signing. To this day, the treaties are the subject of political and legal disputes among Canadians.

Railways

In the early days of French and British colonization, and in the establishments of the great inland fur trading companies, waterways were by far the most significant means of transportation in the Canadian interior. In fact, waterways continued to be the best means of transportation well into the 19th century. Navigated by steamboats (after 1809), barges, sailboats, and canoes, these waterways also served as frozen highways for wagons and sleds during the long winter months.

A monumental undertaking, the Canadian Pacific Railway came to life in 1878 as part of the National Policy aimed at increasing immigration and western settlement in Canada's frontier and discouraging importation of American goods. As part of its mandate, the railway was granted right of use to existing publicly funded railway lines, a land grant of 10 million hectares, and a subsidy of $25 million for new construction.

The Canadian Pacific Railway included a cast of international engineers, financiers, and labourers. The initial grant of $25 million was supplemented over and over again to cover the enormous costs of building more than 5,000 kilometres of track. The cost in human life was also high. Hundreds of labourers—many of them Chinese workers who came to Canada specifically to work on the railway—lost their lives over the nearly seven years of construction.

In November 1885, the last spike was driven at Craigellachie, British Columbia. The Canadian Pacific Railway, connecting Montreal and Vancouver, was open for business, and the National Policy had become a national reality.

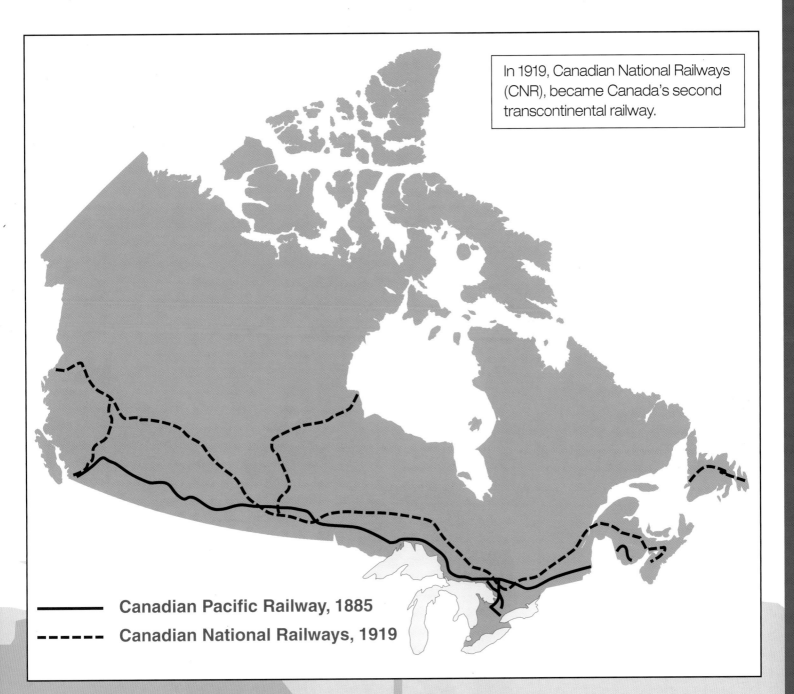

In 1919, Canadian National Railways (CNR), became Canada's second transcontinental railway.

——— Canadian Pacific Railway, 1885
- - - - Canadian National Railways, 1919

The Klondike Gold Rush

The last great North American gold rush of the 19th century began on August 16, 1896, in the Klondike region of present-day Yukon Territory. By 1897, news of Klondike gold on Bonanza Creek had spread worldwide, and by 1898 miners were pouring into the region. Despite difficult terrain and brutally cold weather, prospectors braved mountain passes, generally approaching Bonanza Creek from the wild Alaskan side. They were often met at the Canadian border by the Mounties, who instituted order in the gold rush boom. Estimates vary, but at least $50 million in gold was mined before international businesses took over mining operations in 1900. Although the population went from boom to bust, the gold rush prompted the Canadian government to recognize the area. In 1898, the Yukon Territory was created.

The Mounties

In 1874, a group of red-coated recruits rode out of Dufferin, Manitoba, to address illegal activities in Canada's western territory (now Alberta). Called the North-West Mounted Police, the force was created by an Act of Parliament in 1873. In 1920, it was renamed the Royal Canadian Mounted Police.

The Council of Empire and the Imperial Defence Conference

A movement toward a "trade" rather than a military empire had inspired Queen Victoria to sign the British North America Act of 1867 (see p. 44). However, a call to imperial loyalty was renewed in the closing days of the 1800s, due in large part to British actions in South Africa against the Boers (see below). Britain's Colonial Secretary urged the colonies—including Canada—to join in a Council of the Empire, complete with closer military and commercial ties.

Although Canada never joined the Council of the Empire, Canadians were called on to serve in the Queen's armies in 1899 during the Boer War. The Boer War was fought in South Africa between the British colonists there and the original Dutch settlers in the area, the Boers. The Canadian government did not agree to join the British in their African conflict by sending paid or conscripted Canadian troops. However, they did equip and send an army of more than 7,000 volunteers.

In 1909, Britain again put pressure on Canada to join British imperial causes. At issue were the Kaiser and the gathering storm clouds of a German war in Europe. At the Imperial Defence Conference, Britain suggested that Canada build a navy that, in turn, could be mustered by Britain to fight in her wars. Canada resisted the suggestion, but eventually joined Britain's military effort against Germany in World War I.

World War I (1914–1918)

World War I was the first war that involved countries from all over the world. The war was fought by the **Allies** against the **Central Powers**.

Allies	Central Powers
Belgium	Germany
Britain (including its colonies)	Austria-Hungary
France	Bulgaria
Italy (from 1915)	The Ottoman Empire
United States (from 1917)	

The Canadian contingent that shipped out on October 3, 1914, is still the largest armed force to cross the ocean. It consisted of 33,000 men, 7,000 horses, and 144 pieces of artillery in 32 ships.

Britain declared war on Germany and Austria-Hungary on August 4, 1914. Because Canada was part of the British Empire, Canadians were also at war. By October 3, 1914, Canadian troops were on their way to the battlefields of Europe.

In the trenches

CAUSES OF WORLD WAR I

1 The industrial countries of Europe were very competitive. Some had large world empires that their leaders wanted to expand.

2 To protect themselves, countries formed alliances. These alliances proclaimed that if one nation were attacked, the other nations would defend it. France, Russia, and Britain had an alliance called the Triple Entente. Germany, Austria-Hungary, and Italy had signed the Triple Alliance in 1882.

3 The war was triggered by the assassination of the Austrian Archduke Franz Ferdinand in Sarajevo, Serbia, a small country in central Europe. In response, Austria-Hungary attacked Serbia.

4 The alliances brought many countries into the war. Russia came to the aid of Serbia. Germany then declared war on Russia. France declared war on Germany. Germany attacked Belgium. Britain and Canada entered the war to help Belgium and France.

5 Many Czechs, Slovaks, and other Slavic peoples, seeking freedom from Austria-Hungary, fought for the Allies.

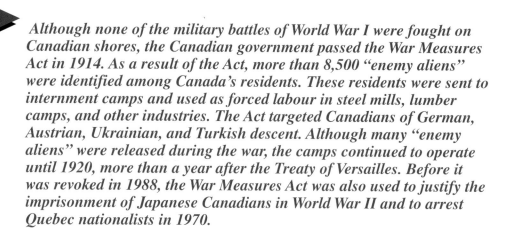

Although none of the military battles of World War I were fought on Canadian shores, the Canadian government passed the War Measures Act in 1914. As a result of the Act, more than 8,500 "enemy aliens" were identified among Canada's residents. These residents were sent to internment camps and used as forced labour in steel mills, lumber camps, and other industries. The Act targeted Canadians of German, Austrian, Ukrainian, and Turkish descent. Although many "enemy aliens" were released during the war, the camps continued to operate until 1920, more than a year after the Treaty of Versailles. Before it was revoked in 1988, the War Measures Act was also used to justify the imprisonment of Japanese Canadians in World War II and to arrest Quebec nationalists in 1970.

Canadians in Battle

Canadians distinguished themselves in several battles during World War I, including:

Ypres, April 22–May 24, 1915
More than 6,000 Canadian troops are dead, missing, or wounded following German chlorine gas attacks and heavy machine gun fire. This battle is the first major use of gas on the Western Front, and the Canadians' bravery in the face of the deadly gas seals their reputation as courageous and able troops.

Somme, July 1–late November, 1916
The First Newfoundland Regiment alone loses 722 of its 790 troops at Beaumont-Hamel in a daytime advance into no man's land.

Vimy Ridge, April 9–14, 1917
After the failure of British and French forces to capture the ridge, Canadian troops, representing all four divisions of the Canadian Corps and led by Canadian officer Arthur Currie, sweep Germans from the ridge at Vimy. By April 14, Canadians gain more ground, more guns, and more prisoners than any previous British offensive in the war. Nearly 3,600 Canadians die in the battle.

Passchendaele, October 26–November 30, 1917
Canadians make a series of attacks on German positions in Belgian marshland and lose more than 15,000 men in the effort to capture five square kilometres. Later, six Canadians receive the Victoria Cross—Britain's highest military honour—for their bravery at Passchendaele.

 Almost a quarter of Britain's fliers in World War I were Canadians. Of the top 26 British aces, with 30 or more kills, 10 were from Canada.

RESULTS OF WORLD WAR I

The Treaty of Versailles, which was signed on June 28, 1919, had the following conditions:

1 Germany was forced to give up territory and colonies to France, Belgium, Denmark, and Poland.

2 To prevent Germany from starting another war, the size of its army was reduced. It was forbidden to have submarines or aircraft.

3 Germany accepted responsibility for starting the war and was penalized 132 billion gold marks in damages to other nations. Today, that's the equivalent of over $370 billion.

4 The League of Nations, an association of countries with the goal of promoting international co-operation, was formed (see p. 61). The League of Nations went on to make disputed territories, like Palestine, protectorates. All German interests in these areas were cut off.

Canada on the World Stage

Although still a part of the British Empire, Canada insisted on signing the Treaty of Versailles that put an end to World War I. This act signalled Canada's intention to set its own political course in the years to come. Canada was given its own seat in the General Assembly of the newly formed League of Nations and later joined the International Labour Organization independent of Britain.

Chapter 7
Canada Comes of Age (1919–1945)

The years between World War I and World War II were years of social reform in Canada. More and more, the country took charge of its affairs. In this period, much of the population moved from rural areas to cities, and the economy shifted from agricultural to urban and industrial.

Government policies were written to address the social changes brought about by the shifts in the population and economy. For example, policies addressed such areas of life as education, religion, health, and poverty. The Canadian labour movement worked to improve conditions for workers in Canada's factories and workplaces. Women won the vote. The Great Depression inspired government programs to help poor and struggling citizens. And another World War tested the population.

Unions and the Labour Movement

A union is a group of workers who come together to bargain with business owners. Management represents the business owners' interests. Because groups of workers acting together have more power to win their demands than one individual, printers, stonecutters, machinists, shoemakers, tailors, and others formed craft and trade unions in the early 1800s.

The growth of trade unions in Canada followed the ups and downs of the economy in general. At various points in labour history, the purpose of unions appeared to be more to protect existing wage levels and jobs than to make demands for higher wages and improved conditions in the workplace.

Gradually, the unions gained strength. In 1872, a union of Toronto printers went on a **labour strike** to have their workday limited to nine hours. As a group, they refused to work until their employers met their demands. The strike was successful, and thereafter Canada's union movement was given legal recognition by the Canadian government. By 1883, the Trades and Labour Congress was organized, a forerunner to the present-day Canadian Labour Congress.

The Winnipeg General Strike in 1919 involved 94 of 96 unions. The strike, which lasted six weeks, resulted in a riot, but established the principle of collective bargaining to address labour disputes.

After the end of World War I, nearly half a million men returned to swell the ranks of Canadian workers. Inspired by the theories of German philosopher Karl Marx, these workers hoped to create their own "workers' paradise" in Canada. Through their unions, these workers made increasingly vocal and radical demands. The government responded by banning several organizations, especially among the unions in the West, and the radical versus conservative lines fractured the Trades and Labour Congress (TLC).

By 1919, the more radical unions had broken away from the TLC altogether. They met to discuss the creation of one revolutionary industrial union, the One Big Union (OBU). To reach their goals, the OBU movement encouraged labour strikes. By 1920, the OBU movement numbered nearly 50,000 Canadians.

Before World War I, Canadian unions represented fewer than 150,000 workers. Today the Canadian Labour Congress represents more than 2.5 million workers.

Women's Rights

The Canadian arm of the Women's Christian Temperance Union (WCTU) was founded in 1874 to campaign for temperance (abstaining from the consumption of alcohol) among individuals and prohibition (the banning of alcoholic beverages by the government). They also promoted reforms such as the vote for women (**suffrage**) and allowances for non-working mothers.

In an 1898 referendum, Prime Minister Wilfrid Laurier declared voter turnout too low, and the majority won by the pro-temperance voters too small, to enact Prohibition. The matter of "demon rum" then became a provincial affair. Between 1901 and 1916, every province but Quebec enacted laws prohibiting the sale of alcohol. By 1930, almost every province had repealed the laws. But for the WCTU, all was not lost. The matter of women's rights was still not settled. It took until 1940 for women across the country to gain the right to vote in all provincial elections.

On May 24, 1918, the Canadian Elections Act passed, giving women in Canada the right to vote in federal elections.

TIMETABLE OF WOMEN AND THE VOTE

1916	Manitoba, Saskatchewan, and Alberta
1917	British Columbia and Ontario
1918	Canada (federal) and Nova Scotia
1919	New Brunswick, Yukon Territory
1922	Prince Edward Island
1925	Newfoundland
1940	Quebec
1951	Northwest Territories (this was because it was the first time elected members were included in council)

 The right of Canadian women to vote was not entirely won with the Canadian Elections Act of 1918. In Quebec, women were denied the right to vote in provincial elections until 1940. What's more, voting rights were withheld from Aboriginal women— as they were from all Aboriginal people in Canada—until 1960!

The Persons Case

Emily Murphy, also known as Janey Canuck, was a writer and suffragette who made her home in Alberta. At a time when women were considered little more than the property of their husbands or fathers, Murphy worked to improve women's status in Canada. In 1917, she organized enough public pressure to force the Alberta legislature to pass a law protecting the property of married women. She also worked on reforming the treatment of women in the male-dominated courtrooms of Edmonton. She even went so far as to suggest a separate court be created for women.

The Alberta government agreed, and appointed Murphy the judge of the newly approved women's court. But no sooner did Murphy take her seat on the bench than her qualifications to serve as judge were challenged. Based on the language in the BNA Act (see p. 44), only qualified "persons" could hold such jobs as legislator or judge. According to British common law, women were not considered "legal persons" in matters involving rights and privileges.

Although Alberta's courts overturned the challenge, the "persons" issue remained unsettled throughout Canada. Murphy had worked hard over the years since her appointment to press what came to be called the Persons Case, and in 1927 she challenged Ottawa to settle the matter once and for all. She noted in the language of the BNA Act a rule that stated that any five citizens petitioning together could request of the Supreme Court of Canada a hearing on any provision of the BNA Act. Murphy got busy and enlisted some help with her cause. Joining her to form the "Famous Five," as we now call them, were Henrietta Edwards, co-founder of the National Council of Women, and Members of Alberta's Legislative Assembly Nellie McClung, Louise McKinney, and Irene Parlby. The Court responded in 1928: women were not legally persons.

The Famous Five did not rest, however, and took their case to the British Privy Council in London. On October 18, 1929, it overturned the Supreme Court of Canada's decision. Since then Canadian women have been considered fully and legally "persons."

The Great Depression (1929–1939)

Canada enjoyed boom years during the 1920s. The economy grew rapidly. But the Roaring Twenties came to a sudden halt when the stock markets in New York, Toronto, Montreal, and other cities around the world, came crashing down in October 1929.

After the crash, Canadian workers and companies suffered greatly. Prices deflated and businesses declined, leading to massive unemployment. Families' savings disappeared and many lost their homes. Communities in the prairie provinces that relied on farming, mining, and logging were hardest hit. To add insult to injury, a seven-year drought caused crop failures on top of the initial collapse in the wheat market.

Also known as the Dirty Thirties, the era of the Great Depression lasted until 1939. The onset of World War II created a need for goods and services to equip the world for battle, and a new boom in jobs and the economy resulted, ending the Depression.

CAUSES OF THE GREAT DEPRESSION AND ITS IMPACT ON CANADA

1 The business boom of the 1920s made people overly confident. They invested their money in risky stock deals and borrowed money on credit. When stock prices crashed, they lost all their savings.

2 Canada was suffering an international trade deficit. It brought in more goods from foreign countries than it exported into their markets.

3 Machines had begun to replace human workers in many factory jobs.

4 A devastating drought on the prairies wiped out Canada's wheat crops.

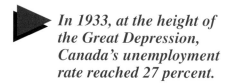

In 1933, at the height of the Great Depression, Canada's unemployment rate reached 27 percent.

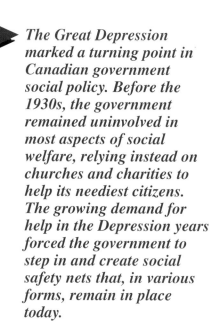

The Great Depression marked a turning point in Canadian government social policy. Before the 1930s, the government remained uninvolved in most aspects of social welfare, relying instead on churches and charities to help its neediest citizens. The growing demand for help in the Depression years forced the government to step in and create social safety nets that, in various forms, remain in place today.

World War II (1939–1945)

World War II resulted from German, Italian, and Japanese conquests of neighbouring nations in the late 1930s. Two days after the German invasion of Poland on September 1, 1939, Britain and France declared war on Germany. One week later, Canada declared war.

The Allies

Britain

Canada

India

Australia and New Zealand

China

France

Soviet Union (from 1941)

United States (from 1941)

The Axis

Germany

Italy

Japan

Soviet Union (until 1941)

CAUSES OF WORLD WAR II

1 Dictators in Germany, Japan, and Italy promoted a fanatical national pride. They also took over the government and installed themselves as the sole heads of state. To support their regimes, they created powerful police networks that enforced their ideas of government.

2 The Treaty of Versailles that ended World War I left Germany poor and its national pride injured.

3 The Axis powers wanted to conquer their neighbours. Japan wanted a "New World Order" in Asia, Italy wanted to rule much of Africa, and Germany wanted to rule Europe. Each invaded other countries and replaced those governments with military dictatorships.

More than 100,000 of the one million Canadians and Newfoundlanders who served in World War II were either killed or wounded.

Canadians in Battle

Canadians contributed in many ways to the great efforts in World War II, including:

Hong Kong, December 18–25, 1941	Nearly 2,000 Canadians are among British forces in Hong Kong as Japanese troops invade. More than 500 ill-prepared and poorly equipped Canadian soldiers die either in battle or in Japanese prisoner of war camps as a result of the battle.
Dieppe, August 19, 1942	Soldiers from the Royal Regiment of Canada are asked to storm the beachhead at Dieppe, leaving the 2nd Canadian Infantry to take the fire in a nine-hour battle. Of the 6,000 allied troops in the conflict, 5,000 are Canadians.
Ortona, December 20–27, 1943	American, British, and Canadian forces land in Sicily and fight their way up Italy before reaching a deadlock against German forces near the town of Ortona. Canadian 1st Division troopers fight house to house, with casualties numbering over 2,200 before a bloody victory is won.
Juno Beach, Normandy, June 6, 1944	More than 14,000 Canadian troops land in the Allied Invasion on D-Day. In the year following the invasion, Canadian troops advance, clearing the coast and liberating the Netherlands in early 1945.

Results of World War II

1 Thirty to forty-five million people lost their lives.

2 It was the most expensive war in history, costing more than one trillion dollars and leaving extensive property damage.

3 Millions of people in Europe and Asia lost their homes. Some were unable to return to their home countries. They needed help to start new lives.

4 The extermination of European Jews by Hitler and the Nazis resulted in forty percent of the world's Jewish population being killed. Six million Jews, Gypsies, disabled people, homosexuals, and political opponents lost their lives in this Holocaust (see p. 60).

5 Japan wrote a new constitution and formed a more democratic government.

6 Germany was divided into two different countries: East Germany (under the influence of the Soviet Union) and West Germany (a federal republic under the influence of the United States, France, and Britain).

7 The United States and the Soviet Union became the chief world powers, and their differences led to the Cold War (see p. 63), which lasted for the next forty years.

8 The United Nations was formed.

Into the Modern Era (1945–)

Chapter 8

More than six million European Jews were murdered because of Hitler's efforts to wipe out Jewish people. Following the war, several hundred thousand Jews were released by Allied troops from the concentration camps where they had been held by the Nazis. Many of these concentration camp survivors sought refuge in North and South America. However, Canadian immigration policy was opposed to people of Jewish religion and ethnicity settling in the country. In contrast to the United States and South American countries, where nearly 300,000 Jewish Holocaust survivors were welcomed, fewer than 8,000 Jewish refugees were admitted to Canada during the post-war era.

During the post-war years, modern Canada emerged on its own terms. On the homefront, the years from 1945 to the present have been marked by the creation of a new Constitution and Charter (see p. 65). On the world stage, Canada has emerged as a founder of the United Nations and a voice for peace in world affairs.

The New Canadians: Immigration After World War II

Between 1945 and 1969, two million people immigrated to Canada. These new Canadians changed the fundamentally British and French origins of the population to include a variety of ethnicities and races present in the population today.

The early waves of immigration were largely from Europe because, until the 1960s, immigration policy limited the numbers of Asians, Africans, and Caribbean islanders who sought to make their lives in Canada. In the years immediately following World War II, tens of thousands of Britons, Italians, Germans, Dutch, and Poles tried to rebuild their war-shattered lives in Canada. Among these immigrants were British war brides who met and married Canadian soldiers overseas. Later, in the 1950s, more than 35,000 Hungarian refugees fled Soviet authority in their home country to start new lives in Canada.

To support the massive migration to its shores, a variety of Canadian religious and cultural organizations—including Roman Catholics, Baptists, Lutherans, and Mennonites—formed the Canadian Christian Council for the Resettlement of Refugees (CCCRR). Other immigrants arrived to live with relatives. Still others—approximately 160,000 Europeans called "displaced persons" (people with no homes to go back to)—signed contracts with the government, promising two years of manual labour in exchange for the right to live in Canada.

Since the 1960s, an influx of immigration from all continents of the world has added to the post-war immigrants. Together these new Canadians have created Canada's modern multiethnic national culture. This culture is particularly apparent in Ontario and British Columbia, provinces favoured as immigrant destinations for the employment opportunities in the many factories, mines, and service industries located there.

The Citizenship Act of 1946

On January 1, 1947, the Citizenship Act of 1946 was enacted and made law.

Although immigration policy at the time of the Citizenship Act was hardly tolerant of non-Europeans, the Act itself set Canada apart from its identification with Britain. Rather than recognize new Canadians as British subjects, the Act described citizens instead as Canadians first and foremost.

The United Nations

Canada was one of the founding nations of the United Nations (UN). Officially established in 1945 with the aim of maintaining world peace and security, the UN was formed with input from the allied nations and world leaders who had defeated the Axis powers in World War II (see p. 57). Once a member of the League of Nations (see p. 52), Canada had long recognized the significance of international cooperation in the prevention of war and conflict, and joined with the United States, Britain, France, and the Soviet Union, among other nations, to create this new international body with its headquarters in New York City.

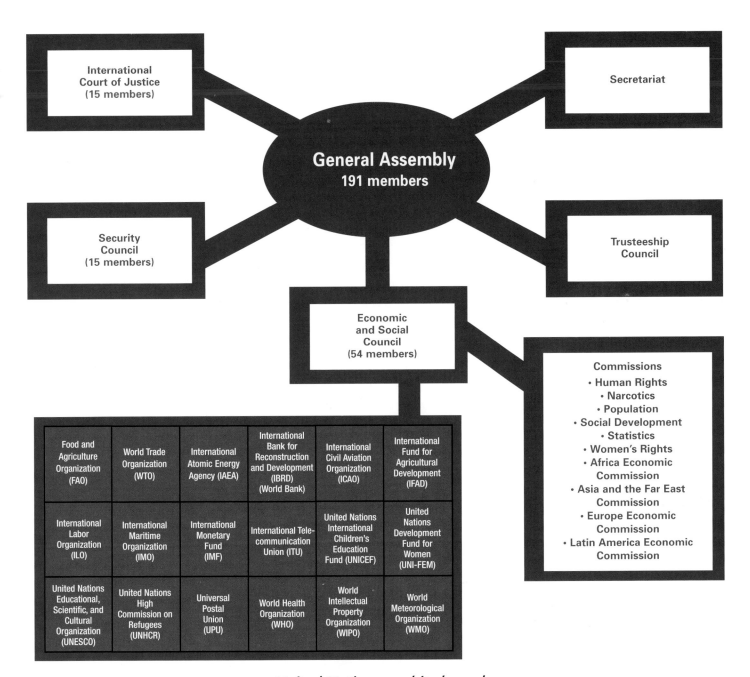

United Nations and its branches

The UN is made up of several branches. Among the most significant of these branches are:

The **General Assembly**, which is made up of all the members of the United Nations. Each member has one vote. The General Assembly can make recommendations, but cannot give orders to act militarily.

The **Security Council**, which is made up of 15 members. There are five permanent members—the United States, Britain, France, Russia, and the People's Republic of China. The other ten members are elected to two-year terms. Only the Security Council can order the United Nations to take military actions. To do this, nine of the 15 members must vote for action. All five permanent members must also vote in favour of the action. Any one of the permanent members can veto, or reject, a call for action.

The **International Court of Justice**, which meets in The Hague in the Netherlands, is made up of 15 judges who decide cases by majority vote. When nations submit their cases to the court, they agree to accept its decision.

The **Secretariat**, which consists of the secretary general and his or her staff. It is responsible for the administrative work of the United Nations. The secretary general is appointed by the General Assembly for a five-year term.

The Korean War (1950–1953)

At the end of World War II, Korea was divided into two countries: Communist-ruled North Korea and democratic South Korea. The Soviet Union occupied the North, and the United States occupied the South. The division was the 38th parallel, an imaginary line that was in the centre of Korea. The Korean War began on June 25, 1950, when North Korea invaded South Korea. The United Nations (see p. 61) demanded that the North Koreans withdraw, but was ignored. The UN declared North Korea the aggressor and sent military aid to South Korea.

This was the first war in which the UN played a military role. Calling it a "police action," the UN asked its member nations to give military aid to South Korea. Canada was among 16 nations that sent combat forces to the South Koreans, and among 41 nations that sent military equipment, food, and other supplies. Among the Canadian contributions were eight ships of the Royal Canadian Navy, air power from the Royal Canadian Air Force, and ground troops. In all, over 26,000 Canadians served in the Korean War. More than 1,500 were wounded or killed.

The Korean War ended on July 27, 1953, when the UN and North Korea signed an armistice, or cease-fire agreement. A permanent peace treaty between South Korea and North Korea has never been signed. The war ended with no declared victor. To this day, the countries are divided and tensions between them remain high.

The Cold War and NATO

The Cold War was a war of words, not guns. It was a struggle between the democratic nations of the West—including Canada, the United States, Britain, and France—and the nations allied with the former Soviet Union.

The Soviet Union was ruled by a communist dictatorship in which all its people were supposed to share in the nation's wealth and government. In fact, dictators and the Communist Party tightly controlled every part of Soviet peoples' lives. Both the Soviet countries and the Western democracies wanted to protect their interests and gain allies around the world. This led to the creation of the North Atlantic Treaty Organization (NATO), a coalition of Western countries committed to resisting Communism. The Soviets responded by forming the Warsaw Pact with their allies.

The Cold War lasted from the end of World War II until the 1980s, when the Berlin Wall was torn down in 1989, and Soviet communism ended when the USSR was dissolved in 1991.

The Suez Crisis

In 1956, Egyptian president Gamal Abdel Nasser seized control of the Suez Canal, a major thoroughfare for international shipping and trading. Nasser's actions prompted a military response from a coalition of three countries: Britain, France, and Israel. The United Nations worked to resolve the confrontation and to avoid any increase in hostility in the area. Led by the Canadian delegation, the UN created a plan to insert multinational peacekeeping forces between the Egyptian and allied combatants. The plan proved successful, leading to a reduction in tension in the area and the avoidance of all-out war.

Since the crisis, Canadians have emerged as a "middle power" and as an international voice for peace and compromise among the world's nations.

 The Canadian delegation to the United Nations during the Suez Crisis was led by Lester Pearson, who was awarded the Nobel Peace Prize in 1957 in honour of his leadership and achievement in peacekeeping. Pearson became the first Canadian to win the prestigious prize.

The Quiet Revolution

From World War II until 1960, French-speaking Quebec was governed by the *Union Nationale* party. The party was led by Maurice Duplessis until his death in 1959. Under the *Union Nationale*, French-speaking interests were protected largely through traditional channels like the Roman Catholic Church, and appealed primarily to French-Canadian pride. Many historians and social commentators have described its policies as oppressive to free speech and democratic ideals. By 1960, the seeds of discontent with the *Union Nationale* led to the election of a Liberal government in Quebec, with Jean Lesage as premier.

The years that followed were dubbed by the press as *la revolution tranquille*, the Quiet Revolution. During this time, Quebec's population, economy, culture, and politics moved away from conservative religious, local-minded policies to a philosophy of secularism (not governed by church policy) and participation in national politics. The motto *maîtres chez nous*, "masters of our own house," was embraced by many Quebecois and led the province to actively seek protection for francophone rights. The revolution also brought about Quebec's investment in developing provincial industry, particularly hydroelectric energy, and in revolutionizing the educational system. A minority of Quebecois called for the separation of the province from Canada during the Lesage years, and the beginnings of Quebec movements for independence can also be traced to the Quiet Revolution.

The Bill of Rights (1960)

Passed by Parliament in 1960, the Bill for the Recognition and Protection of Human Rights and Fundamental Freedoms (also known as the Bill of Rights) promises all Canadians life, liberty, and personal security. The bill also guarantees freedoms, including the freedom of religion, speech, assembly, and the press.

The Bill of Rights was considered by then Prime Minister John Diefenbaker to be among his greatest accomplishments. However, in reality, the letter of the bill was unenforceable because it was not part of the Constitution, nor did it have any authority within provincial courts.

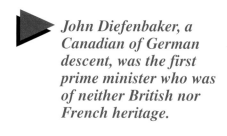

John Diefenbaker, a Canadian of German descent, was the first prime minister who was of neither British nor French heritage.

The Constitution Act (1982)

Until 1982, Canada's constitution was framed in the British North America Act (see p. 44). Although the BNA Act remained a statute of Parliament from 1867, over the years Canadians sought to create a new constitution that better addressed the balance of power between provinces and the federal government, especially as these powers affected taxes, educational programs, and medical care. Also of concern were language rights and the powers of the Supreme Court.

By 1981, nine of Canada's then ten premiers agreed on terms for the new constitution. Although Quebec, as well as women's and Aboriginal peoples' interest groups, objected to aspects of the proposal, the Canada Act passed in March 1982, and formally removed the BNA Act as an official statute. In April, Queen Elizabeth II attended the ceremony in Ottawa celebrating the passage of the Constitution Act into law.

On the whole, the Constitution Act was based on the BNA Act and the several amendments made to it since its enactment in 1867. Some significant amendments were included in this new legislation, but, perhaps most important, the new Constitution recognized, after 115 years of British sovereignty, Canada's complete independence from Britain.

The Charter of Rights and Freedoms

The Charter of Rights and Freedoms is an integral part of the Constitution Act of 1982. The Charter, while in many ways inspired by the U.S. Bill of Rights, offers a far broader and deeper list of personal rights and freedoms than the U.S. document. Among other liberties, it promises equality among all Canadian citizens, no matter what race, ethnicity, religion, sex, age, and mental or physical disability. The Charter also outlines equality for French and English speakers.

Canada

Area: 9,984,670 square kilometres

Population: 32,146,547

Capital: Ottawa

Provinces and Territories:
10 provinces and 3 territories: Alberta, British Columbia, Manitoba, New Brunswick, Newfoundland and Labrador, Northwest Territories, Nova Scotia, Nunavut, Ontario, Prince Edward Island, Quebec, Saskatchewan, Yukon Territory

Independence: July 1, 1867, became a self-governing dominion

December 11, 1931, independence formally recognized

National Holiday:
Canada Day, July 1

Constitution: Consists of the Constitution Act of March 29, 1867, which created a federation of four provinces, and the Constitution Act of April 17, 1982, which transferred formal control over the Constitution from Britain to Canada, and added the Canadian Charter of Rights and Freedoms, as well as procedures for constitutional amendments.

Legal System: Based on English common law, except in Quebec, where the civil law system is based on French law.

Official Languages: English and French

Government: Confederation with parliamentary democracy

Geography

Location: Canada occupies nearly the entire northern half of the continent of North America. Only Alaska and Greenland are not part of Canada. Alaska and the Pacific Ocean border the west, the Atlantic Ocean borders the east. The United States is to the south, with the Arctic Ocean to the north.

Largest Cities: Toronto and Montreal

Land

Natural Regions: Canadian Shield (hard rocky area), the Great Plains (flat, open fields), western cordillera (mountainous area), the Appalachian range, and the St. Lawrence lowlands

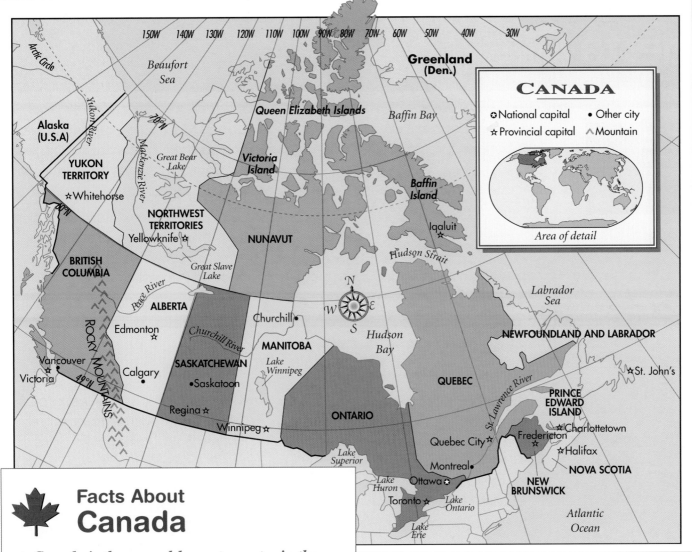

CANADA

- ✪ National capital
- ☆ Provincial capital
- • Other city
- ⋀ Mountain

Area of detail

Facts About
Canada

- *Canada is the second-largest country in the world by area (after Russia), but ranks only 35th in population. Most Canadians live in the southern portion of the country, within a few hundred kilometres of the U.S. border. Much of the rest of Canada is sparsely inhabited.*

- *Coastline is 202,080 kilometres, the longest in the world.*

- *The Canada-United States border is the longest continuous border (6,416 kilometres) between two nations in the world.*

Highest Point: Mount Logan, 5,959 metres

Major Rivers: Mackenzie, St. Lawrence, Nelson, and Columbia Rivers

Major Lakes: Superior, Michigan, Huron, Erie, Ontario, Winnipeg, Great Bear, and Great Slave Lakes

Principal Industries:

Mining/Natural Resource: Iron ore, coal, potash, petroleum, nickel, zinc, molybdenum, uranium, copper, gold, lead, silver, aluminum, timber, fish, wheat, oil, hydroelectric power, and natural gas

Manufacturing: Paper, wood products, transportation equipment, chemicals, and high tech industries such as computer software and aerospace supplies

Agriculture: Wheat, barley, oilseed, tobacco, fruits, vegetables, dairy products, and fish

Service: Business service, banking, education, health care, trade, and communications

Tourism: About three million people visit Canada each year, and 175 million Canadians visit places within Canada, generating jobs and money for the country.

Alberta

Motto: *Fortis et liber*
"Strong and free"

Area: 661,848 square kilometres

Population: 3,201,900

Capital: Edmonton

Origin of Name: Named for Princess Louise Caroline Alberta, fourth daughter of Queen Victoria of Britain

Joined Confederation: September 1, 1905

Flower: Wild Rose

Tree: Lodgepole Pine

Bird: Great Horned Owl

Time Zone: Mountain Standard

Government

Provincial Government: 83-seat elected Legislative Assembly, including the premier and Cabinet

Federal Representation: 28 elected Members of Parliament, 6 Senators

Geography

Location: Westernmost of the three Prairie provinces, Alberta is located in southwestern Canada. It is bordered by British Columbia to the west, Saskatchewan to the east, the Northwest Territories to the north, and the United States to the south.

Largest Cities: Edmonton and Calgary

Land: Mountains, prairies, forests, and southern badlands. The badlands is a dry, rocky area in the southeast.

Natural Regions: Montane cordillera (the Rocky Mountains along the western border), interior plains, taiga plains. Over half of Alberta is covered in forests.

Highest Point: Mount Columbia, 3,747 metres

Major Rivers: Peace River and Athabasca River

Major Lakes: Lake Athabasca, Lake Claire (the largest lake entirely in Alberta)

Principal Industries

Mining/Natural Resources: Oil, natural gas, and coal (largest producer of oil, gas and coal in Canada)

Agriculture: Wheat (second-largest producer in Canada), livestock, and dairy farms

Manufacturing: Paper and wood products

Service: Telecommunications

Tourism: Fourth-largest industry

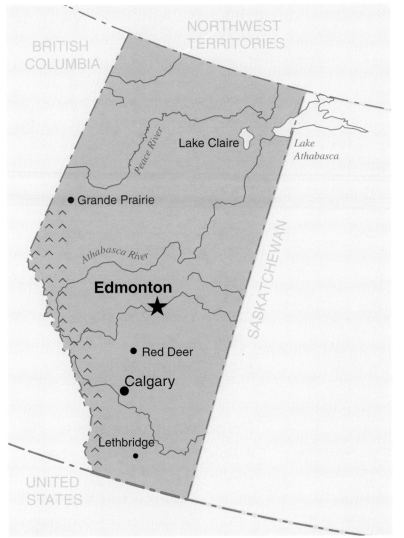

Downtown Calgary

 Facts About
Alberta

- *Oil was discovered at Leduc (near Edmonton) in 1947.*

- *Alberta has the largest area protected as national parks of any Canadian province: Banff National Park (Canada's first national park), Elk Island National Park, Jasper National Park, Waterton Lakes National Park, and Wood Buffalo National Park.*

- *Wood Buffalo National Park is home to about 2,200 endangered wood buffalo.*

- *Alberta is home to five of Canada's 13 United Nations World Heritage Sites, areas designated by the United Nations Educational Scientific and Cultural Organization.*

- *In 1998, Alberta mined its one billionth ton of coal.*

British Columbia

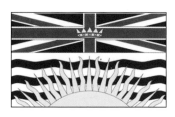

Motto: *Splendor sine occasu* "Splendor without diminishment"

Area: 944,735 square kilometres

Population: 4,196,400

Capital: Victoria

Origin of Name: Named for the Columbia River, which was named for American explorer Robert Gray's ship, the *Columbia*.

Joined Confederation: July 20, 1871

Flower: Pacific Dogwood

Tree: Western Red Cedar

Bird: Stellar's Jay

Time Zone: Pacific Standard

Government

Provincial Government: 79-seat elected Legislative Assembly, including the premier and Cabinet

Federal Representation: 36 elected Members of Parliament, 6 Senators

Geography

Location: The westernmost of Canada's ten provinces and the third largest. The Yukon Territory is to the north, the Pacific Ocean to the west, the United States mainland to the south, and Alberta to the east. Thousands of islands along the west coast, including the Queen Charlotte Islands, are part of the province.

Largest City: Vancouver

Highest Point: Fairweather Mountain, 4,663 metres

Land: Forest, mountains, and coast. Coast mountains in the west, the Columbia Mountains in the centre, the Rocky Mountains in the east, and the Interior Plateau between the coast and the Columbia Mountains.

Natural Regions: Part of Canada's cordillera region. Includes boreal cordillera, Pacific Maritime, montane cordillera.

Major Rivers: Fraser River (one of the longest rivers in Canada) and Columbia River. Both flow into the Pacific Ocean.

Major Lakes: Williston Lake (a man-made lake) and Atlin Lake

Principal Industries

Manufacturing: Pulp and paper products

Mining/Natural Resources: Natural gas (Canada's second-largest producer) and hydroelectricity (Canada's second-largest producer)

Fishing: British Columbia salmon and more than 20 other species of fish (Canada's largest fishing economy)

Tourism

 Facts About
British Columbia

- *British Columbia is the third-largest film and television production centre in North America, after New York and Los Angeles.*

- *In July 2003, Vancouver was selected to host the 2010 Winter Olympic and Paralympic Games.*

Vancouver and marina as viewed from Stanley Park

Manitoba

Motto: *Glorious et liber*
"Glorious and free"

Area: 647,979 square kilometres

Population: 1,170,300

Capital: Winnipeg

Origin of Name: From a Cree name meaning "the place where the spirit speaks"

Joined Confederation: July 15, 1870

Flower: Prairie Crocus

Tree: White Spruce

Bird: Great Gray Owl

Time Zone: Central Standard

Government

Provincial Government: 57-seat elected Legislative Assembly, including the premier and Cabinet

Federal Representation: 14 elected Members of Parliament, 6 Senators

Geography

Location: Manitoba, the eastern-most of the three prairie provinces, lies between Saskatchewan to the west and Ontario to the east, Nunavut to the north and the United States to the south.

Largest City: Winnipeg

Land: Pine, hemlock, and birch forests. Forty-one percent of the province is covered by wetlands and peatlands. Unlike other provinces, Manitoba is comparatively level, generally ranging from 150 metres to 300 metres above sea level.

Natural Regions: Interior plains, Canadian Shield, Hudson Bay Lowlands, and Arctic tundra

Highest Point: Baldy Mountain, 832 metres

Major Rivers: The Churchill River, Nelson River, and the Red River are the three largest rivers. All drain north-east into Hudson Bay.

Largest Lakes: Lake Winnipeg, Lake Winnipegosis, and Lake Manitoba

Principal Industries

Manufacturing: Food, machinery, transportation equipment, metal, clothing, paper, and wood products

Agriculture: Wheat (major crop), barley, canola, flaxseed, oats, and rye. Manitoba is the leading producer of flaxseed, sunflower seeds, buckwheat, and field peas in Canada.

Mining/Natural Resources: Hydroelectricity, nickel, gold, copper, zinc, cadmium, and silver

Fisheries: Freshwater fish

Manitoba Legislature

 ### Facts About
Manitoba

- *Manitoba is known as "the land of 10,000 lakes," since almost one-sixth of the province is made up of freshwater lakes.*

- *Pisew Falls is the second-highest waterfall in Manitoba at 13 metres—just one metre less than Kwasitchewan Falls.*

- *Churchill (in northern Manitoba) is "the polar bear capital of the world."*

New Brunswick

Motto: *Spem reduxit*
"Hope was restored"

Area: 73,435 square kilometres

Population: 751,400

Capital: Fredericton

Origin of Name: Named for the British royal family of Brunswick

Joined Confederation: July 1, 1867

Flower: Purple Violet

Tree: Balsam Fir

Bird: Black-Capped Chickadee

Time Zone: Atlantic Standard Time

Government

Provincial Government: 55-seat elected Legislative Assembly, including the premier and Cabinet

Federal Representation: 10 elected Members of Parliament, 10 Senators

Geography:

Location: New Brunswick is the westernmost of the three Maritime provinces—Nova Scotia, Prince Edward Island, and New Brunswick. New Brunswick lies between Quebec to the northwest, the United States to the south and west, and Prince Edward Island, Nova Scotia and the Atlantic Ocean to the east.

Largest City: Saint John

Land: Forest, mountains, and shoreline (half the province is surrounded by water)

Natural Regions: Appalachian Region, or the Atlantic Maritime region, which is made up of three distinct areas: the Appalachians in the west, the Northumberland coastal plain, and the Atlantic Ocean

Highest Point: Mount Carleton, 817 metres

Major Rivers: Saint John River, Restigouche River, Nepisiguit River and Miramichi River

Major Lakes: Grand Lake, Oromocto Lake, and Magaguadavic Lake

Principal Industries

Manufacturing: Lumber, pulp, paper, wood products, food, fabricated metal, non-metallic mineral products, and machinery

Fishing: Lobster, more than 50 other varieties of fish and shellfish

Agriculture: Dairy products, potatoes (major crop), apples, blueberries, strawberries, and cranberries

Mining/Natural Resources: Lead, zinc, copper, bismuth, gold, zinc, silver, natural gas, oil, coal, and hydroelectricity

Tourism

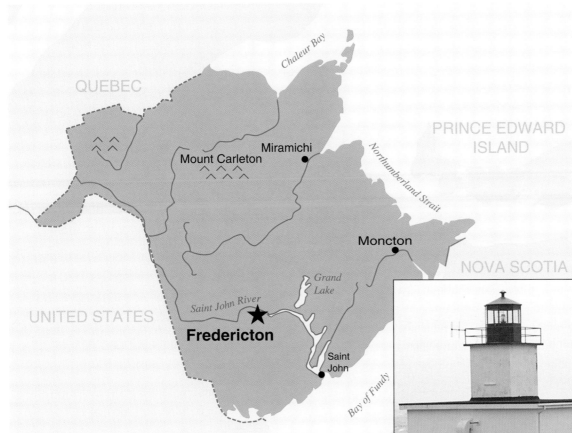

QUEBEC

Chaleur Bay

Miramichi

Mount Carleton

PRINCE EDWARD ISLAND

Northumberland Strait

Moncton

NOVA SCOTIA

Grand Lake

Saint John River

UNITED STATES

Fredericton

Saint John

Bay of Fundy

 ## Facts About
New Brunswick

- *The Bay of Fundy between New Brunswick and Nova Scotia has the world's highest tides (15 metres high).*

- *The first coal in Canada was mined near Grand Lake, New Brunswick, in 1639.*

- *The Saint John River Valley is called the "Potato Belt."*

Lobster traps sitting on the grass near a lighthouse in a New Brunswick harbour.

Newfoundland and Labrador

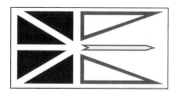

Motto: *Quaerite prime regnum dei* "Seek ye first the Kingdom of God"

Area: 405,212 square kilometres

Population: 517,000

Capital: St. John's

Origin of Names: Named "new founde land" by John Cabot in 1497; Labrador from the Portuguese *Terra del Lavradors*, meaning "land of the small landowners."

Joined Confederation: March 31, 1949

Flower: Pitcher Plant

Tree: Black Spruce

Bird: Atlantic Puffin

Time Zone: Newfoundland Standard Time for Newfoundland; Atlantic Standard for Labrador

Government

Provincial Government: 48-seat elected House of Assembly, including the premier and Cabinet

Federal Representation: 7 elected Members of Parliament, 6 Senators

Geography

Location: The easternmost of Canada's provinces, Newfoundland has two sections: the island of Newfoundland, and Labrador on the mainland. Labrador is bordered by Quebec on the west and the Labrador Sea on the northeast;

Newfoundland is surrounded by the Gulf of St. Lawrence to the west and the Atlantic Ocean to the north, east and south.

Largest city: St. John's

Land: Mountains, forests, lakes and coastline. Much of the interior of Labrador is great plateau. Tundra in the north.

Natural Regions: Canadian Shield and Appalachian Mountain system

Highest Point: Mount Caubvick, 1,652 metres. It's also Quebec's highest point, where it's known as Mont D'Iberville.

Major Rivers: Churchill River, Exploits River, Gander River

Largest Lakes: Smallwood Reservoir, Melville Lake, and Grand Lake

Principal Industries

Fishing: Crab, shrimp (main shellfish), clam, flatfish, turbot, capelin, and mackerel. Aquaculture (fish farming) includes salmon, steelhead trout, and mussels

Manufacturing: Newsprint (main producer in Canada), refined petroleum, processed fish, and seafood

Mining/Natural Resources: Iron, (main producer in Canada), gold, dolomite, limestone, dimension stone, gravel, offshore oil (greatest export), hydroelectricity.

Salvage Harbour in Salvage, Newfoundland. The buildings pictured are fishing stages.

Labrador Sea

Labrador

Smallwood Reservoir

Churchill River

● Goose Bay

Labrador City ●

ATLANTIC OCEAN

Strait of Belle Isle

Notre Dame Bay

Newfoundland

Trinity Bay

Gulf of St. Lawrence

Corner Brook ●

Grand Lake

★ **St. John's**

 Facts About

Newfoundland and Labrador

- *Churchill Falls in Labrador is one of the largest hydroelectric power plants in the world.*

- *The waters off Newfoundland are among the richest fishing grounds in the world. Referred to as banks, these underwater plateaus are home to numerous species of fish. The largest bank is called the Grand Banks. Overfishing has caused a severe decline in the amount of fish in the Grand Banks, especially codfish (see p. 21).*

- *The coastlines of Newfoundland and Labrador contain numerous bays and deep fjords. Just off the coast is the Continental Shelf, an underwater plateau. The Grand Banks is part of the Continental Shelf.*

- *Signal Hill is a high cliff above the harbour at St. John's where Italian inventor Guglielmo Marconi received the first radio message from across the Atlantic Ocean.*

Nova Scotia

Motto: *Munit Haec et Altera Vincit* "One defends and the other conquers"

Area: 53,000 square kilometres

Population: 937,000

Capital: Halifax

Origin of Name: Latin for "New Scotland"

Joined Confederation: July 1, 1867

Flower: Mayflower

Tree: Red Spruce

Bird: Osprey

Time Zone: Atlantic Standard

Government

Provincial Government: 52-seat elected Legislative Assembly, including the premier and Cabinet

Federal Representation: 11 elected Members of Parliament, 10 Senators

Geography

Location: One of the three Maritime provinces, Nova Scotia is attached to mainland Canada by a stretch of land called the Isthmus of Chignecto. It also includes Cape Breton Island, and many smaller islands. Except for the isthmus, it is bordered on all sides by water. The Bay of Fundy is to its west, the Northumberland Strait lies to its north, separating it from Prince Edward Island, and the Atlantic Ocean lies to the east and south.

Largest City: Halifax

Land: Forest and coastline (7,400 kilometres)

Natural Regions: Nova Scotia is part of the Appalachian region, a mountainous region that covers much of eastern North America. It is also part of the Atlantic Maritime region.

Highest Point: White Hill Lake, Cape Breton Highlands, at 530 metres

Major Rivers: Mersey River, Shubenacadie River, and the LaHave River

Major Lakes: Bras d'Or on Cape Breton Island. It is the largest salt water lake in North America.

Principal Industries

Fishing: Lobsters, scallops, haddock, halibut, flounder, and herring. Nova Scotia is the world's largest exporter of lobster. There are also many aquaculture farms that grow Atlantic salmon, mussels and oysters in huge pens that are suspended in shallow sections of the ocean.

Manufacturing: Pulp, paper mills, and sawmills

Mining/Natural Resources: Coal, natural gas, salt, clay, and gypsum. Nova Scotia is North America's largest producer of high-grade gypsum, a mineral used to make things like plasterboard, chalk, and toothpaste.

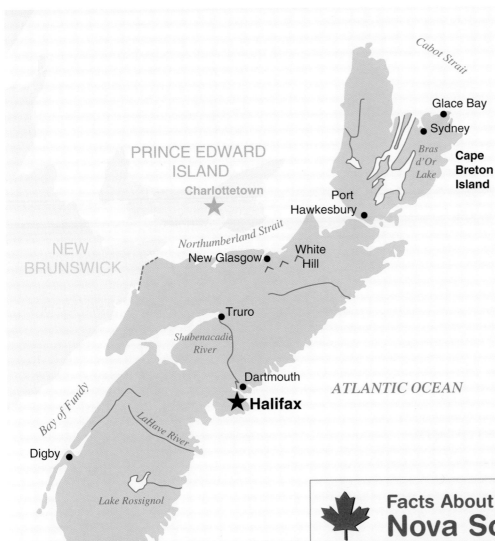

Lighthouse at Peggy's Cove

Agriculture: Livestock, dairy products, apples, and blueberries (largest producer of blueberries in the world)

Tourism: More than one million people visit Nova Scotia each year.

Facts About
Nova Scotia

- *Marconi sent the first wireless (radio) message across the Atlantic Ocean, from Table Head, Cape Breton Island, in 1902.*

- *In 1784, Nova Scotia was split to form two provinces: Nova Scotia and New Brunswick.*

- *The town of Lunenburg was named a United Nations World Heritage site in 1995 in recognition of its remarkably well-preserved architecture dating from the 1700s.*

- *The French built a settlement at Port Royal in 1605. It was the first European settlement in what is now Canada.*

Ontario

Motto: *Ut incepit Fidelis sic permanet* "Loyal it began, and loyal it remains"

Area: 1,068,582 square kilometres

Population: 12,392,700

Capital: Toronto

Origin of Name: From an Iroquoian word "Kanadario" meaning "sparkling water," or "beautiful lake"

Joined Confederation: July 1, 1867

Flower: White Trillium

Tree: Eastern White Pine

Bird: Common Loon

Time Zone: Central and Eastern Standard

Government

Provincial Government: 103-seat elected Legislative Assembly, including the premier and Cabinet

Federal Representation: 106 elected Members of Parliament, 24 Senators

Geography

Location: Quebec is to the east, Manitoba to the west, Great Lakes and the United States to the south, Hudson Bay and James Bay to the north.

Largest City: Toronto (Toronto is also Canada's largest city)

Land: Forests, lakes, and wetlands

Natural Regions: Great Lakes-St. Lawrence Lowlands, Canadian Shield, and Hudson Bay Lowlands. Two-thirds of Ontario is in the Canadian Shield, which is made up of hard rock, forests, and lakes. The lowlands of Hudson Bay and James Bay are mostly wetlands. The Great Lakes-St. Lawrence lowlands contain some of Canada's best farmland.

Highest Point: Ishpatina Ridge, 693 metres

Major Rivers: St. Lawrence River and the Ottawa River

Major Lakes: Ontario contains four of the five Great Lakes—Superior, Huron, Erie, and Ontario. Lake Superior is the world's largest fresh-water lake by area.

Principal Industries

Service: Finance (banking and insurance), information services, real estate

Mining/Natural Resources: Nickel, copper, platinum, palladium, crude oil, cobalt, salt, magnesium, zinc, platinum, gold, silver, natural gas, and hydroelectricity

Manufacturing: Automobiles and auto parts, steel, pulp and paper industry (the second largest in Canada), and building materials. Ontario is Canada's manufacturing leader and produces almost 60% of all exported manufactured goods.

Agriculture: Fruits and vegetables (Canada's leading producer), livestock, dairy farms, vineyards and wineries

Tourism

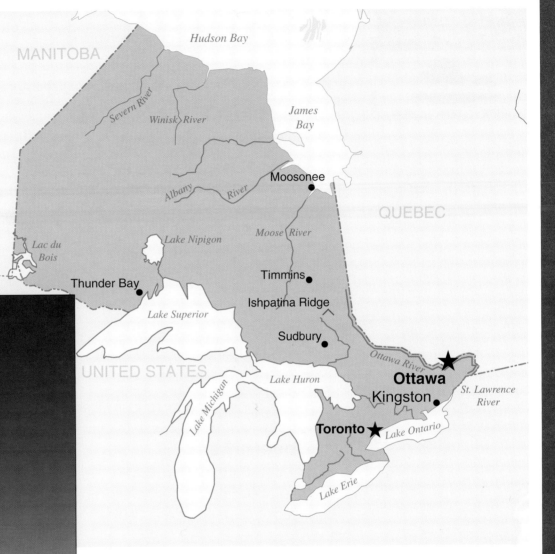

Toronto's CN Tower

Facts About
Ontario

- *Ontario has more than 1,100 public libraries, including the Metropolitan Toronto Library, Canada's largest public library system. Library and Archives Canada and the Parliamentary Library are in Ottawa.*

- *One quarter of Canada's farms are located in Ontario.*

Prince Edward Island

Motto: *Parva sub Ingenti*
"The small under the protection of the great"

Area: 5,655 square kilometres

Population: 137,900

Capital: Charlottetown

Origin of Name: Named "Prince Edward" in 1799 in honour of a son of King George III, who was stationed in Halifax at the time. He was also the father of Queen Victoria.

Joined Confederation:
July 1, 1873

Flower: Lady's Slipper

Tree: Red Oak

Bird: Blue Jay

Time Zone: Atlantic Standard Time

Government

Provincial Government:
27-seat elected Legislative Assembly, including the premier and Cabinet

Federal Representation:
4 elected Members of Parliament, 4 Senators

Geography

Location: Prince Edward Island (PEI) sits in the Gulf of St. Lawrence on Canada's east coast. The Northumberland Strait separates PEI from New Brunswick and Nova Scotia, with Nova Scotia to the south and east and New Brunswick to the south and west.

Largest City: Charlottetown

Land: Rolling plains, beaches, iron-rich (red) sandstone soil. PEI is part of the Appalachian Mountain chain that covers much of the east coast of North America.

Natural Regions: The Atlantic Maritime and Appalachian Mountain.

Highest Point: Springton in Queens County, 152 metres

Major Rivers: None. The island's main supply of water is from groundwater.

Major Lakes: None, however, several streams have been dammed to create small lakes.

Principal Industries

Manufacturing: Processed agricultural and fishing products, pulp, and lumber

Agriculture: Potatoes (main crop), fruits and vegetables, and grains

Fishing: Lobsters, mussels, crab, herring, and mackerel. Also, Irish moss, a type of seaweed

Tourism: More than 1.2 million tourists visit the province each year.

 ### Facts About
Prince Edward Island

- *Charlottetown hosted the historic Charlottetown Conference on September 1, 1864, an event that led to the formation of a Canadian union (see p. 43).*

- *Tourists come from around the world to visit Green Gables House, home and museum of the Anne of Green Gables books by L. M. Montgomery.*

- *Confederation Bridge joins New Brunswick and Prince Edward Island. The bridge was opened in 1997 and is almost 13 kilometres long.*

Confederation Bridge, connecting Prince Edward Island to New Brunswick

Quebec

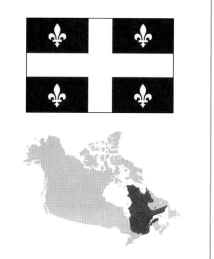

Motto: *Je me souviens*
"I remember"

Area: 1,540,680 square kilometres

Population: 7,542,800

Capital: Quebec City

Origin of Name: From an Algonquian word meaning, "where the river narrows," referring to the St. Lawrence River.

Joined Confederation: July 1, 1867

Flower: Blue Flag Iris

Tree: Yellow Birch

Bird: Snowy Owl

Time Zone: Eastern Standard

Government

Provincial Government: 125-seat elected National Assembly, including the premier and Cabinet

Federal Representation: 75 elected Members of Parliament, 24 Senators

Geography

Location: Canada's largest province, Quebec is bordered by Ontario to the west and south, the U.S. to the south, Hudson Bay to the west, New Brunswick and Labrador to the east, and the Hudson Strait to the north.

Largest Cities: Montreal and Quebec City

Land: Forest, lakes, tundra

Natural Regions: Canadian Shield, St. Lawrence Lowlands and Appalachian Mountains. Over 80% of the province lies in the Canadian Shield, a rocky, forested land with many lakes, Arctic areas (mostly tundra), the taiga and boreal shield (primarily evergreen forest), and mixed woods plains (deciduous and evergreen trees).

Highest Point: Mont D'Iberville in the Torngat Mountains, 1,652 metres

Major Rivers: St. Lawrence, St-Maurice, Saguenay, Ottawa, Manicouagan, Nottaway, Rupert, La Grande, Outaouais, Eastmain, and Koksoak Rivers

Major Lakes: Lake Mistassini, Manicouagan Reservoir

Principal Industries

Mining/Natural Resources: Gold, cement, zinc, stone, copper, sand, gravel, silver, peat, iron ore, and hydroelectricity

Agriculture: Livestock and dairy (largest producer in Canada), fruits, vegetables and maple syrup

Manufacturing: Textiles, food, lumber, pulp and paper products, and aeronautics and space industry

Finance: Banking, insurance, and stock exchange

Tourism

Service Industries

Facts About
Quebec

- *Quebec City is North America's only fortified city.*

- *In 1985, it was designated as a United Nations Educational Science and Cultural Organization World Heritage City.*

- *In 1959, the St. Lawrence Seaway was opened. The seaway links the Great Lakes and the Atlantic Ocean.*

- *Quebec is the largest province, with 15.5% of the total area of Canada. It has the second-largest population.*

- *The hydroelectric plant near James Bay is the largest engineering project in Canadian history. It's one of the largest hydroelectric systems in the world.*

- *Quebec has more fresh water than any other province, with more than one million lakes and waterways.*

Quebec City along the St. Lawrence River

Saskatchewan

Motto: *Multis e gentibus vires* "From many peoples, strength"

Area: 651,900 square kilometres

Population: 995,058

Capital: Regina

Origin of Name: From a Cree word meaning "swiftly flowing river"

Joined Confederation: September 1, 1905

Flower: Western Red Lily or Prairie Lily

Tree: White Birch

Bird: Sharp-Tailed Grouse

Time Zone: Central Standard

Government

Provincial Government: 58-seat elected Legislative Assembly, including the premier and Cabinet

Federal Representation: 14 elected Members of Parliament, 6 Senators

Geography

Location: One of the three Prairie provinces, located between Alberta to the west, and Manitoba to the east, the Northwest Territories to the north, and the United States to the south.

Largest City: Saskatoon

Land: Forest, agricultural flatlands, and tundra

Natural Regions: The Canadian Shield, made up of rocky areas, coniferous forest, and some tundra; the Interior Plains and waterways.

Highest Point: Cypress Hills, 1,392 metres

Major Rivers: North and South Saskatchewan, Assiniboine, and Churchill Rivers

Major Lakes: Wollaston Lake, Cree Lake. Lake Athabasca (shared with Alberta) and Reindeer Lake (shared with Manitoba) are the largest. There are more than 100,000 lakes, rivers, and marshes in the province.

Principal Industries

Manufacturing: Wood, paper and pulp products, food processing

Agriculture: Wheat, canola, rye, oats, barley, flaxseed, and livestock

Mining/Natural Resources: Oil and natural gas (second-largest producer), uranium, coal, and potash

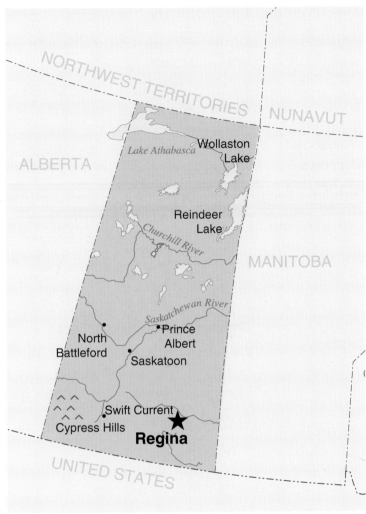

Facts About
Saskatchewan

- *Regina, the capital city, is the home of the Royal Canadian Mounted Police academy.*

- *Saskatchewan has more road surface than any province in Canada: over 200,000 kilometres.*

The Saskatchewan Legislative Building

Northwest Territories

Motto: None

Area: 1,346,106 square kilometres

Population: 42,800

Capital: Yellowknife

Origin of Name: Original name of the land acquired from the Hudson's Bay Company in 1870 was Rupert's Land and the North-Western Territory.

Joined Confederation: July 15, 1870

Flower: Mountain Avens

Tree: Tamarack

Bird: Gyrfalcon

Time Zone: Mountain Standard

Government

Territorial Government: 19-seat elected Legislative Assembly, including the premier and Cabinet

Federal Representation: 1 Member of Parliament, 1 Senator

Geography

Location: The Northwest Territories are bordered by the Yukon Territory to the west, Nunavut to the east, the Arctic Ocean to the north, and British Columbia, Alberta, and Saskatchewan to the south.

Largest City: Yellowknife

Land: Mountains, tundra, barren land, and forest

Natural Regions: Canadian Shield (lakes, rocky areas, tundra, and barren land), boreal forest (mixed evergreens and deciduous), Arctic and subarctic, (permafrost, or permanently frozen soil)

Major Rivers: Mackenzie, Back, Thelon, Coppermine, and Dubawnt

Major Lakes: Great Slave Lake and Great Bear Lake

Principal Industries

Mining/Natural Resources: Lead, zinc, gold, tungsten, iron, diamonds, petroleum, and natural gas

Trapping and Fishing

Tourism

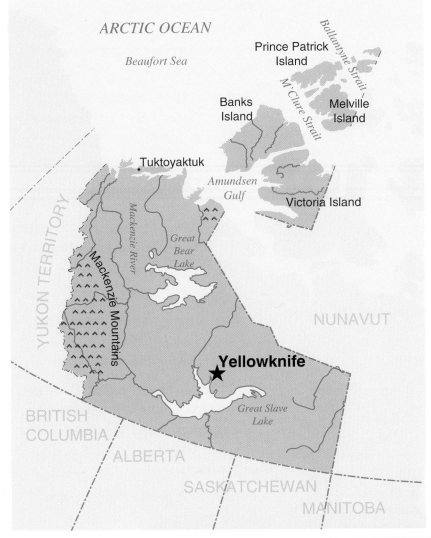

ARCTIC OCEAN

Beaufort Sea

Prince Patrick Island

Ballantyne Strait

Banks Island

M'Clure Strait

Melville Island

Tuktoyaktuk

Amundsen Gulf

Victoria Island

YUKON TERRITORY

Mackenzie River

Great Bear Lake

Mackenzie Mountains

NUNAVUT

Yellowknife ★

BRITISH COLUMBIA

Great Slave Lake

ALBERTA

SASKATCHEWAN

MANITOBA

Facts About
the Northwest Territories

- *Yukon, Alberta, Saskatchewan, plus parts of Manitoba, Ontario, Quebec, and Nunavut were all once part of the Northwest Territories.*

- *Mackenzie River is the longest river in Canada, and Great Slave Lake is the deepest lake in North America.*

- *Wood Buffalo National Park is home to the wood bison and a nesting site for the endangered whooping cranes.*

- *The Mackenzie Delta, the Mackenzie River drainage area, is Canada's largest fresh water delta.*

Bison

Nunavut

Motto: *Nunavut Sanginivut* [Inuktitut] "Nunavut, our strength"

Area: 2,093,190 square kilometres

Population: 29,600

Capital: Iqaluit

Origin of Name: Means "our land" in the Inuit language of Inuktitut.

Joined Confederation: April 1, 1999

Flower: Purple Saxifrage

Tree: None

Bird: Rock Ptarmigan

Time Zone: Central Standard

Government

Territorial Government: 79-seat elected Legislative Assembly, including the premier and Cabinet

Federal Representation: 36 elected Members of Parliament, 1 Senator

Geography

Location: Nunavut is bordered by the Northwest Territories to the west, and Hudson Bay to the southeast. It extends north to the North Pole.

Largest City: Iqaluit

Land: Tundra and frozen subsoil where moss, grasses, and a few shrubs grow

Natural Areas: Arctic permafrost, subarctic tundra, Canadian Shield. Mountainous areas, few trees. The land is covered with sheets of ice and water pools.

Highest Point: Barbeau Peak, 2,616 metres

Major River: The Sylvia Grinnel River

Principal Industries

Service: Especially government

Mining/Natural Resources: Lead, silver, zinc, iron, gold, copper, diamonds, oil and gas

Facts About
Nunavut

- *Nunavut is the largest territory and occupies nearly one-fifth of the land in Canada. It was originally part of the Northwest Territories. Nunavut is made up of mainland and numerous islands in the Arctic Ocean, including Baffin Island and Ellesmere Island.*

- *Ellesmere Island National Park Reserve is Canada's northernmost park.*

- *The village of Alert is the northernmost community in Canada, with a permanent population of five people. The average forecast high in January is -28.2°C and in July is 1.7°C. Alert experiences 24-hour-a-day daylight for four months of the year, and round-the-clock darkness for four months of the year.*

Fishing, Hunting and Trapping: Turbot, shrimp, and Arctic char are the main fish. Seal, caribou, and white fox.

Manufacturing: Fish and meat processing

Arts and Crafts: The Inuit are known for their arts, especially soapstone sculptures.

Tourism

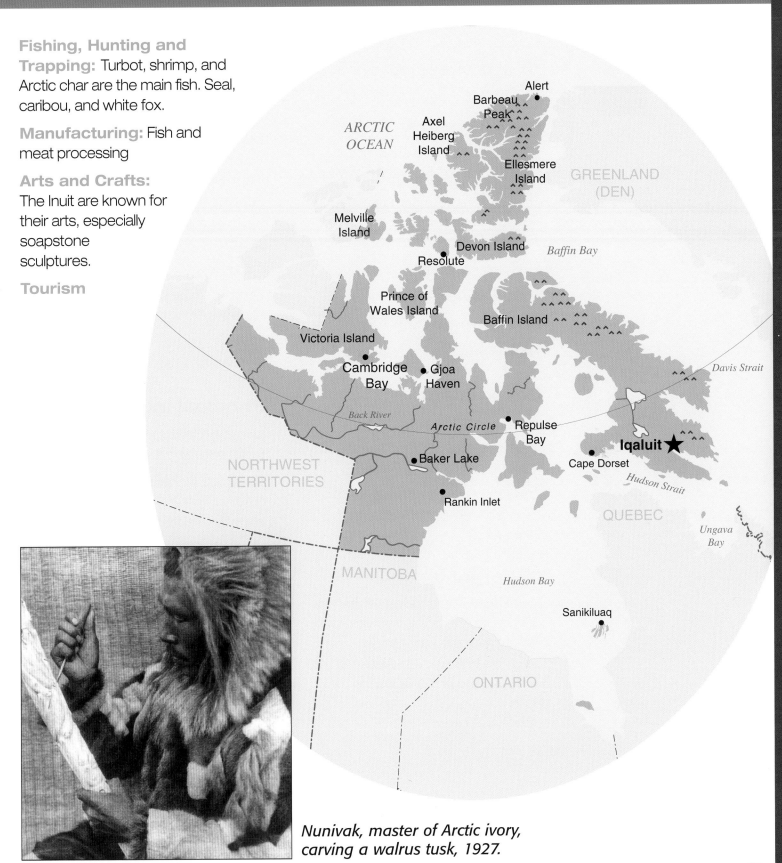

ARCTIC OCEAN

Alert

Barbeau Peak

Axel Heiberg Island

Ellesmere Island

GREENLAND (DEN)

Melville Island

Devon Island

Baffin Bay

Resolute

Prince of Wales Island

Baffin Island

Victoria Island

Cambridge Bay

Gjoa Haven

Davis Strait

Back River

Arctic Circle

Repulse Bay

Iqaluit ★

NORTHWEST TERRITORIES

Baker Lake

Cape Dorset

Hudson Strait

Rankin Inlet

QUEBEC

Ungava Bay

MANITOBA

Hudson Bay

Sanikiluaq

ONTARIO

Nunivak, master of Arctic ivory, carving a walrus tusk, 1927.

Yukon Territory

Motto: None

Area: 482,443 square kilometres

Population: 31,200

Capital: Whitehorse

Origin of Name: From the Native word "Yu-kun-ah" meaning "great river"

Joined Confederation: June 13, 1898

Flower: Fireweed

Tree: Sub-Alpine Fir

Bird: Common Raven

Time Zone: Pacific Standard

Government

Territorial Government:
18-seat elected Legislative Assembly, including premier and Cabinet

Federal Representation:
1 elected Member of Parliament, 1 Senator

Geography

Location: The smallest territory in Canada, bordered by the Northwest Territories to the east, British Columbia to the south, Alaska to the west, and the Arctic Ocean to the north.

Largest City: Whitehorse

Land: Mountains and plateaus, tundra, forests and coastlands

Natural Regions: Western cordillera, the great mountain chain that forms the western margin of North America; boreal forest, and the Arctic coastal plain.

Highest Point: Mount Logan, 5,959 metres (highest mountain in Canada)

Major Rivers: The Yukon, Klondike, Peel, Pelly, Porcupine Rivers

Major Lakes: Kluane, Teslin, Bennett and Laberge Lakes

Principal Industries

Mining/Natural Resources: Gold, lead, zinc, tungsten and silver

Fishing: Northern pike, Arctic grayling, rainbow and lake trout, whitefish, salmon, and Arctic char

Manufacturing: Fish packing and lumber.

Hunting/trapping: Beaver, lynx, wolverine, muskrat, and fox

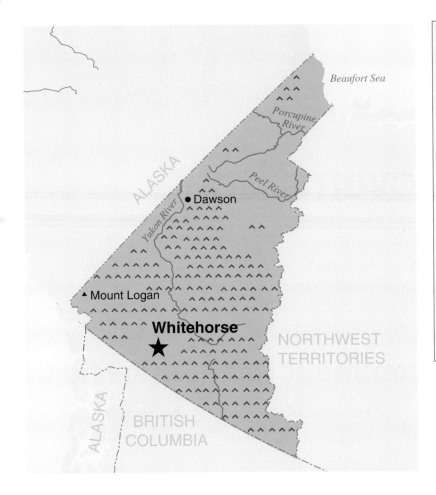

Facts About
Yukon Territory

- *The Alaska Highway, which runs through British Columbia, the Yukon, and Alaska, was built in 1942. Its 2,451 kilometres of roadway were laid in only eight months and twelve days.*

- *In 1979, the Dempster Highway was completed. It is an all-weather road that crosses the Arctic Circle.*

- *The Klondike Gold Rush of 1897 brought many people to the Yukon, but by the early 1900s the gold was nearly depleted and most people left the territory (see p. 48).*

Gravel Lake on the Klondike Loop is an important wetland for migratory birds in spring and fall.

Chapter 1 The Federal Government

Government in Canada has two basic levels: federal and provincial. The federal government is a central government that controls common national matters. The provincial government oversees matters within the province. In addition, municipal governments are responsible for regional and local matters.

Some Government Responsibilities

Federal	Provincial	Municipal
Armed Forces	Education	Law enforcement (local)
Copyright	Provincial roads	Fire department (local)
International Trade	Water and sewage	Water and sewage (local)
Health and welfare	Marriage permits	Animal control
Passports	Energy	Taxes (local)
Federal elections	Natural resources (forestry, mining, etc.)	Recycling
Aboriginal affairs	Provincial parks	
Internet		

Head of State

Queen Elizabeth II is the formal head of the Canadian government. Because she lives in Britain, an appointed Governor General represents the Queen on the federal level, and Lieutenant Governors represent her in each of the provinces. The territories have Territorial Commissioners instead of Lieutenant Governors. However, the commissioners report to the federal government rather than the Crown.

Canada's Parliamentary System

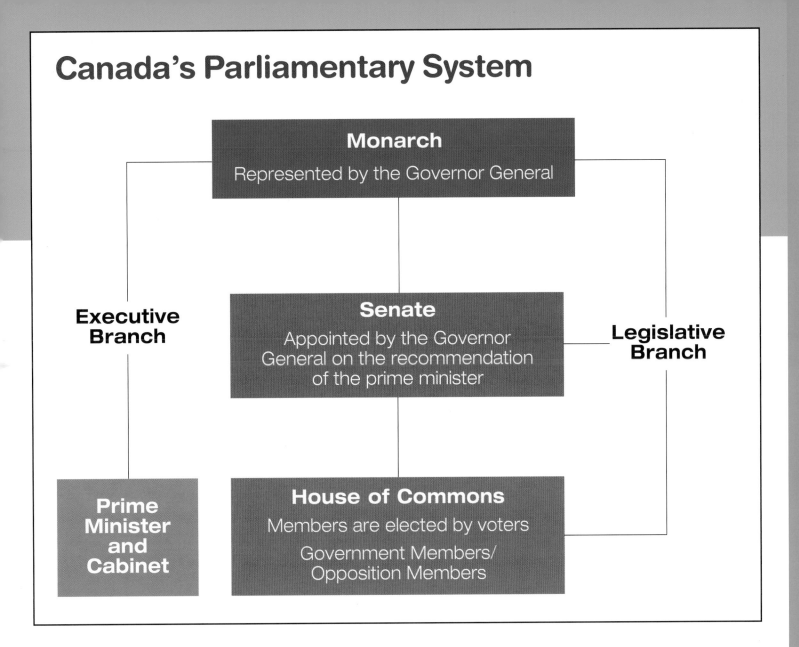

Monarch
Represented by the Governor General

Executive Branch

Legislative Branch

Senate
Appointed by the Governor General on the recommendation of the prime minister

Prime Minister and Cabinet

House of Commons
Members are elected by voters
Government Members/ Opposition Members

The Legislative Branch

Parliament is the legislative branch of the federal government. It is made up of the Monarch, the House of Commons, and the Senate. Parliament meets at the summons of the Monarch, and no federal or provincial bill becomes law without Royal Assent (through the Monarch's representative).

The two legislative branches of the government are the Senate and the House of Commons.

 The term "Parliament" also describes the official time during which Members of Parliament and Senators meet in one or more sessions to conduct government business: from a general election until the prime minister asks the Governor General to dissolve it and call another general election.

The Senate

The Senate is also referred to as Canada's Upper House. The Senate is appointed by the federal government, not elected by the people. Senators are appointed by the Governor General on the recommendation of the prime minister. Senate seats are based on region.

One of the main goals of the Senate is to review legislation from the House of Commons. It can veto (or reject) bills or ask for amendments before granting approval. The Senate can also originate bills, except those that require any spending of public money. No bill can become law unless passed by the Senate.

The Senate also has standing committees that provide in-depth studies of major federal programs, such as health care and other public issues that affect the nation.

The **Speaker** is the presiding officer of the Senate. The Governor General, on the recommendation of the prime minister, appoints the Speaker.

Qualifications for Senate

- Must be a citizen of Canada
- Must be at least 30 years of age
- Must live in the province or territory appointed
- Must own land worth at least $4,000 in the represented province
- Must own assets of at least $4,000

The Senate

The Senate currently has 105 members.

- 24 from the Maritime provinces
    - 10 from Nova Scotia
    - 10 from New Brunswick
    - 4 from Prince Edward Island
- 24 from Quebec
- 24 from Ontario
- 24 from the Western provinces
    - 6 each from Manitoba, Saskatchewan, Alberta, and British Columbia
- 6 from Newfoundland and Labrador
- 1 each from the Territories

The House of Commons

The House of Commons is also known as Canada's Lower House. Canadian voters elect members of the House of Commons. Members of the House are also referred to as Members of Parliament. Each member is elected by and represents the people in his or her electoral district (also called a *riding*).

The House of Commons is the major federal law-making body. Established when the British North America Act of 1867 (see p. 44) created the Dominion of Canada, the House of Commons was set up similarly to the British House of Commons. More powerful than the Senate, it is the body responsible for the laws of the land. Although Senate approval is necessary to pass legislation, only the House can pass laws imposing taxes or the spending of public money.

Government leadership is responsible solely to the House of Commons. The prime minister stays in office only as long as he or she is supported by the majority of seats in the House.

The presiding officer of the House of Commons is known as the Speaker. He or she is elected by secret ballot by the House after each general election. The Speaker's responsibilities are to be impartial and non-partisan (not favouring any political party), to control procedure and order while the House conducts its business, and to manage the House staff.

Seats in the House of Commons are distributed among the provinces according to population, as determined by the most recent census. Members are voted in by general election for a limited term. They hold office until Parliament is dissolved, or for a maximum of five years. Members can be re-elected in the next election.

The House of Commons

The House currently has 308 members.

- 106 from Ontario
- 75 from Quebec
- 36 from British Columbia
- 28 from Alberta
- 14 each from Manitoba and Saskatchewan
- 11 from Nova Scotia
- 10 from New Brunswick
- 7 from Newfoundland and Labrador
- 4 from Prince Edward Island
- 1 each from the Northwest Territories, Nunavut, and the Yukon Territory

The Prime Minister and Cabinet

The prime minister is the head of Canada's federal government. The Governor General officially appoints the prime minister after his or her party has won more seats than any other party in an election. There is no fixed term of office for the prime minister.

The prime minister chooses the members of the Cabinet, a group of people who help him or her run the country. The members of the Cabinet are usually Members of the House of Commons, but sometimes Senators are asked to join. By custom, every province should, if possible, have at least one Cabinet Minister.

The number of Cabinet posts is set by the prime minister, usually based on legislative goals. The number of Cabinet positions in the twentieth century never exceeded 40 and usually numbered in the 30s.

Prime Ministers of Canada

Name	Term of Office
Paul Martin	2003 —
Jean Chrétien	1993 to 2003
Kim Campbell	1993
Brian Mulroney	1984 to 1993
John Turner	1984
Pierre Trudeau	1980 to 1984
Joe Clark	1979 to 1980
Pierre Trudeau	1968 to 1979
Lester B. Pearson	1963 to 1968
John Diefenbaker	1957 to 1963
Louis St. Laurent	1948 to 1957
William Lyon Mackenzie King	1935 to 1948
Richard B. Bennett	1930 to 1935
William Lyon Mackenzie King	1926 to 1930
Arthur Meighen	1926
William Lyon Mackenzie King	1921 to 1926
Arthur Meighen	1920 to 1921
Sir Robert Borden	1911 to 1920
Sir Wilfrid Laurier	1896 to 1911
Sir Charles Tupper	1896
Sir Mackenzie Bowell	1894 to 1896
Sir John Thompson	1892 to 1894
Sir John Abbott	1891 to 1892
Sir John A. Macdonald	1878 to 1891
Alexander Mackenzie	1873 to 1878
Sir John A. Macdonald	1867 to 1873

The Party System

The party system plays an important role in the government of Canada. During an election, more emphasis is placed on the party system than on individuals. For example, the people do not elect the prime minister. Instead, the prime minister is normally an elected member of the House of Commons who becomes prime minister because he or she is the leader of the majority party.

The **majority party** is the party that has won the majority, or the greatest number of seats in Parliament, in an election. The leader of the majority party is appointed prime minister by the Governor General. The majority party is also referred to as the Government.

The party with the second largest number of seats is known as the Official Opposition. Its party leader becomes the Leader of the Opposition. A **minority government** is in power when the opposing parties combined hold more seats than the Government.

Parties are physically separated in the Parliament seating arrangement. On one side of the aisle is the Government, and on the other side is the Opposition. The prime minister and the Cabinet sit in the front row. The Official Opposition leader sits directly across the floor.

 A political party is a group of people who share the same ideas about how to run the government. They work together to try to win the majority, or most number of seats, in Parliament.

CANADA'S MAJOR POLITICAL PARTIES

- Liberal Party of Canada (founded 1867) – liberal

- Conservative Party of Canada (founded 2003) – conservative

- The New Democratic Party (founded 1961) – social democratic

- Bloc Québecois (founded 1990) – Quebec sovereignist, social democratic

- The Green Party (founded 1983) – green/ecological

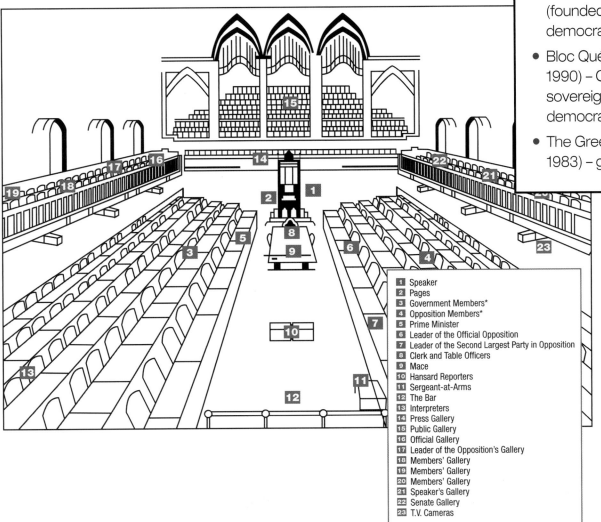

1. Speaker
2. Pages
3. Government Members*
4. Opposition Members*
5. Prime Minister
6. Leader of the Official Opposition
7. Leader of the Second Largest Party in Opposition
8. Clerk and Table Officers
9. Mace
10. Hansard Reporters
11. Sergeant-at-Arms
12. The Bar
13. Interpreters
14. Press Gallery
15. Public Gallery
16. Official Gallery
17. Leader of the Opposition's Gallery
18. Members' Gallery
19. Members' Gallery
20. Members' Gallery
21. Speaker's Gallery
22. Senate Gallery
23. T.V. Cameras

THE LEGISLATIVE PROCESS (HOW A BILL BECOMES LAW)

The following chart shows how a bill becomes law. Either the House of Commons or the Senate can propose a bill, and they go through a similar process. Both must adopt the bill in identical form. The bill must then receive Royal Assent before it becomes law.

1. Introduction and First Reading. A bill must be formally introduced to the House, where it is given a number, printed, and distributed. No debate is allowed at this time.

2. Second Reading and Referral to a Committee. A second reading is introduced and then the bill is referred to a committee. Debate begins but no amendments, or changes, may be made.

3. Committee Stage. The committee examines the bill, holds hearings, and submits a report recommending that the bill be either accepted (with or without changes) or rejected.

4. House Review/Report Stage. The House reviews the committee's work on the bill and allows all members of the House to propose and vote on further amendments.

5. Third Reading. The third reading is the final consideration of the bill. A vote is held. If the bill is approved, it is sent to the other House, where the process begins again.

6. Review. The second House reviews the bill in a manner similar to the first House. However, any amendments made by the second House must be considered by the first, which can accept, reject, or further modify amendments. The bill must be adopted in identical form by both Houses.

7. Royal Assent. This is the procedure by which the representative of the Crown—the Governor General or a deputy—approves the bill. It then becomes an Act of Parliament and the bill becomes law.

Canada's Judicial System

The judicial system is made up of courts and judges who interpret and apply the laws of the land, whether passed by the federal government, provincial legislature, or a local municipality.

The judicial branch of the government has four levels: the Supreme Court, the Federal Court, the Superior Courts, and the Provincial Courts.

Judicial independence is essential. The Canadian Judicial Council is a regulating body made up of chief justices from various courts who hear complaints about federally appointed judges.

The Court System

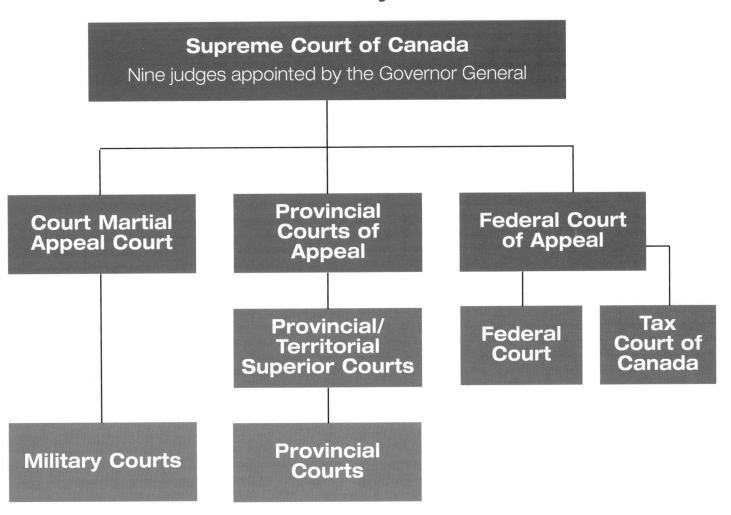

Supreme Court of Canada
Nine judges appointed by the Governor General

Court Martial Appeal Court

Provincial Courts of Appeal

Federal Court of Appeal

Provincial/Territorial Superior Courts

Federal Court

Tax Court of Canada

Military Courts

Provincial Courts

The justices of the Supreme Court of Canada are referred to as "The Honourable (full name) Judge of the (name of court) of Canada," and the Chief Justice as "The Right Honourable." The Chief Justice holds the Right Honourable title for life.

SUPREME COURT

The Supreme Court of Canada is the highest court. Established in 1875 by the Supreme Court Act and located in Ottawa, it hears cases from other courts of law.

The Supreme Court consists of nine judges, one of whom is the Chief Justice. They are appointed by the Governor-in-Council (the Governor General). At least three judges must be from Quebec in recognition of the Quebec civil law system, which differs from that of the other provinces of Canada. The rest of the judges are appointed from other regions of the nation.

The Supreme Court hears appeals from lesser courts on civil and criminal cases. It also makes and interprets decisions on the Constitution, federal and provincial legislation, and the powers of the government. Supreme Court rulings, or judgments, are the final authority for all legal decisions.

FEDERAL COURT OF CANADA

The Federal Court of Canada was established in 1971. It replaced the Exchequer Court of Canada. In 2003, it was broken down into two courts: the Federal Court and the Federal Court of Appeal. These specialized courts hear cases for and against the federal government, including matters of federal legislation, from transportation to immigration, patents, copyrights, and Maritime cases. They also have limited criminal jurisdiction.

Federal Court judges are appointed by the federal government.

Trial by jury: The Canadian Charter of Rights and Freedoms allows individuals accused of serious crimes to be tried by a jury (group of people) or by a judge. The judge alone does sentencing (punishment).

SUPERIOR COURTS OF THE PROVINCES AND TERRITORIES

Each province and territory has its own Superior Court. These courts hear cases concerning a broad range of civil and criminal matters. Their decisions can be appealed to the Supreme Court of Canada.

The federal government appoints Superior Court judges.

PROVINCIAL COURTS

With the exception of Nunavut, every province and territory has a provincial/territorial court. The provincial and territorial courts deal with most criminal offences and civil offences. They also oversee traffic violations, money claims, and offences committed by young people. Some of the courts at this level are subdivided, for example, the Drug Treatment Court program, or youth courts. Nunavut uses the Nunavut Court of Justice, which is Canada's only single level trial court—meaning it has combined the provincial/territorial court with the territorial Supreme Court.

The provincial governments appoint judges in these courts.

Canadian Citizenship

If you were born in Canada, then you are a Canadian citizen. If you come from another country and want to become a Canadian citizen, then you must have lived in Canada for at least three out of the four years prior to applying for citizenship. You must know English or French, the official languages of Canada. It is required that you be able to speak English or French well enough to communicate. Citizenship also requires that you learn about Canada's history, geography, and political system, as well as the rights and responsibilities of citizenship. The parents of children under the age of 18 can apply on their children's behalf.

A Canadian citizen can participate freely and equally in government. Citizens have the right to vote in elections and hold office. Many of the rights of Canadian citizens came about recently. The Citizenship Act was passed in 1947. Prior to that, people living in Canada were officially classified as British subjects. This was the beginning of the status of Canadian citizen, which meant that citizens would now have automatic right of entry into Canada. It also provided for some rights for women, particularly that married women would be treated independently. Previously, their legal status was linked to their husbands.

In 1977, the Citizenship Act was revised to make citizenship more accessible to immigrants, and to grant equally, to people from all countries, the right to become Canadian citizens.

Citizenship

To be eligible for Canadian citizenship

- You must be 18 years of age or older to apply
- You must be in Canada legally as a permanent resident

You cannot become a citizen if:

- you are in prison, on parole or on probation;
- in the past four years, you were in prison, on parole or on probation for a year or more;
- you were convicted of an indictable offence or crime, or an offence under the Citizenship Act in the three years preceding your application;
- you are currently charged with an indictable offence or crime, or an offence under the Citizenship Act;
- you are under a removal order and are not currently allowed to be in Canada;
- you are under investigation for a war crime or a crime against humanity; or
- your Canadian citizenship has been taken away (revoked) in the past five years.

Chapter 2

Cultural Preservation

ONE NATION, TWO LANGUAGES

Canada has two official languages: English and French. Both languages have been spoken in Canada for nearly four centuries, and are recognized in the Constitution of 1867. However, it was the Official Languages Act of 1969 (revised in 1988) that set about to ensure equal rights and privileges for both languages in all federal institutions.

Bilingualism, or the ability to speak two languages fluently, has a long history in Canada. The English and the French have lived together in Canada since the 1600s. The Constitution Act of 1867 recognized both languages as the languages of the government and the courts. The federal government has even appointed a Commissioner of Official Languages who reports directly to Parliament and is responsible for promoting and protecting the use of both languages.

All individuals living in Canada have a right to federal government services in English or in French. All federal laws must be enacted in both languages, and all citizens have the right to appear before federal courts in either English or French. Plus, each province or territory is responsible for providing language education for English and French in elementary and secondary schools.

English

Welcome

French

Bienvenue

ABORIGINAL PEOPLE AND SELF-GOVERNMENT

Almost 4.5 percent of Canada's population, that is 1.2 million Canadians, is of Aboriginal ancestry.

Canada's constitution recognizes three groups of Aboriginal people: First Nations, Métis, and the Inuit. First Nations peoples encompasses many of Canada's First Peoples (see p. 5), and represents many original Aboriginal groups.

The British first recognized Aboriginal peoples in the Royal Proclamation of 1763. This document stated that the Crown was responsible for the well being of Aboriginal peoples and forbade the dismantling of their lands. However, for many years the Canadian government often refused to acknowledge this responsibility. As a result, Aboriginal populations were moved and some, like the Beothuk, were wiped out.

Over the years, the government has begun to acknowledge that Aboriginal people in Canada have a right to self-government, an issue that Aboriginal leaders have insisted upon. These groups want to solve their own problems and control their own culture. The Royal Proclamation originally paved the way, and in the 1950s, the Canadian government began passing legislation that enabled self-government for Aboriginal peoples.

Modern Timeline of Aboriginal Self-Government

1951: Revisions to the Indian Act give Aboriginal peoples more control over their own affairs. However, it is not until 1958 that Aboriginal bands are allowed control over their funds.

1960: Aboriginal Canadians are allowed to vote in federal elections without losing their tax-exempt status under the Indian Act.

1968: Quebec is the last province to grant provincial voting power to Aboriginal peoples.

1969: A government report (called a White Paper) proposes the repeal of the Indian Act, which would remove Aboriginal peoples' special status. But the proposal is dropped, and today the Indian Act, the Constitution, and various treaties determine the legal status of Aboriginal people.

1982: As part of the Constitution Act of 1982, Section 35 states that: "The existing aboriginal and treaty rights of the Aboriginal peoples of Canada are hereby recognized and affirmed." In the Act, "Aboriginal peoples of Canada" includes the Métis and Inuit as well as Canada's First Nations people.

1983: The Penner Report recommends that Aboriginal peoples be recognized as a distinct order of government within the Canadian federation, and that processes that lead to self-government be pursued.

1984: The Cree-Naskapi Act of Quebec becomes Canada's first legislation for Aboriginal self-government.

1994: The Yukon First Nations Self-Government Act, Bill C-34, is granted Royal Assent.

1995: The federal government formally launches a new process for negotiating Aboriginal self-government, based on the recognition of the inherent right to self-government under the Constitution.

1999: The Nunavut Land Claims Agreement results in the territory of Nunavut being created with a great number of self-governing powers for the Inuit.

Today: Land claim settlements continue and will continue for some time. One of the recent disputes is over the extraction of natural resources on Aboriginal lands.

Index